Terrorism and War

Terrorism and War

HOWARD ZINN

Edited by Anthony Arnove

AN OPEN MEDIA BOOK

SEVEN STORIES PRESS
New York • Toronto • London • Sydney

ISBN: 1-58322-493-9

9 8 7 6 5 4 3 2 1

Series editor: Greg Ruggiero

Cover photo: A U.S. Air Force B-1B Lancer drops bombs while on a combat mission in support of strikes on Afghanistan, December 2001. (Courtesy USAF/Getty Images)

Printed in Canada.

CONTENTS

Maps 6

A Note on the Text 8

1. 9-11 9

2. Searching for Common Ground 27

3. A Peaceful Nation? 50

4. The Need for Dissent 57

5. War on Civilians 78

6. The Logic of War 92

7. Not in Our Name 99

Acknowledgments 121

APPENDIX A: Excerpts of the Geneva Protocols 123

APPENDIX B: Suggestions for Further Reading 125

APPENDIX C: Antiwar Organizations and Resources . . 127

Notes 132

Index 144

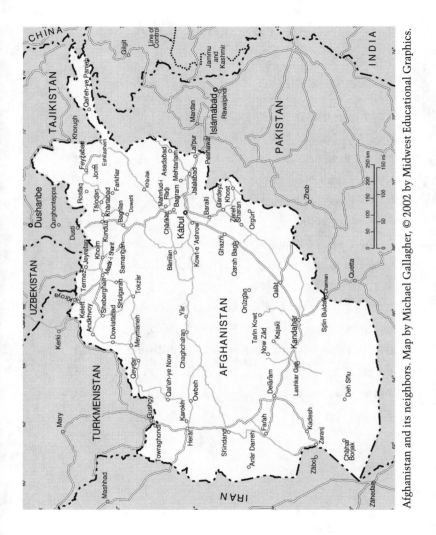

Afghanistan and its neighbors. Map by Michael Gallagher, © 2002 by Midwest Educational Graphics.

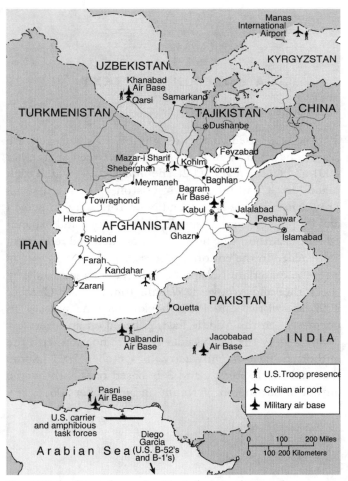

Key U.S. military bases in Central Asia during the war on Afghanistan. Map by Michael Gallagher, © 2002 by Midwest Educational Graphics.

A NOTE ON THE TEXT

This book is based on a series of interviews with Howard Zinn conducted by Anthony Arnove between September 2001 and late January 2002. The interviews—which took place in Cambridge and Boston, Massachusetts; Providence, Rhode Island; and New York City, in person and by phone—were then edited by Arnove and expanded by the author. The notes and more detailed references were added in the editorial process.

Some material in chapter 5 is based on a joint talk by the author and Arnove in Washington, D.C., in October 2002 at Politics and Prose bookstore. One passage in chapter 1, on the Middle East, is based on an interview conducted by the Media Education Foundation with the author at Boston University in October 2001. Some material in chapters 1 and 3 is based on a talk by the author in Burlington, Vermont, in November 2001.

1

9-11

How do you respond to those who support a military solution to the horrific attacks of September 11?

We must understand the pain and anguish that people feel. We can understand, too, the cry for punishment and revenge. But we mustn't let that immediate emotional reaction govern what we do, which should be based on a thoughtful assessment of how we can prevent further violence—whether by terrorists or governments.

The continued expenditure of more than $300 billion for the military every year has absolutely no effect on the danger of terrorism. If we want real security, we will have to change our posture in the world—to stop being an intervening military power and to stop dominating the economies of other countries. According to a 1997 Defense Science Board report, "Historical data show a strong correlation between U.S. involvement in international situations and an increase in terrorist attacks against the United States."[1] "Involvement" is a euphemism for military and covert intervention. We have huge military bases in countries around the world, which the U.S. government is now rapidly expanding, and this inevitably leads to conflict.[2]

What Bush is offering us now as the way to combat terrorism is just what other presidents—Reagan, Clinton, both parties—have offered before: the pursuit of dominance over whole areas of the world. The horror of the terrorist attacks we experienced on September 11 is something that people in other parts of the world—Southeast Asia, Iraq, Yugoslavia—have experienced as a result of our bombings, of terrorism carried out by people we have backed and armed. Knowing this should have a sobering effect on any desire to continue with military solutions.

How do you respond to the feeling that "we must do something"?

You must do something. I agree. But that shouldn't become, "You must do something—therefore, bomb." Is that the only possible thing you can do if you must do something?

You go to war because you want to do something fast. You use violence because you don't want to wait. You don't want to work conflicts out. You don't want to use your mind, your intelligence, your wit. You don't want to use those capacities that a human being is especially endowed with.

Howard Zinn

Medical students take the Hippocratic oath. The first rule is, "Do no harm." I think that is wise counsel. But in bombing Afghanistan, we are doing great harm. Some people have said that we're not killing that many people. The Pentagon says it doesn't know how many people we're killing. The truth is, they don't care. In fact, you can't believe the government. The few reports on civilian deaths that come through the filter of media control are only a tiny fraction of the true figures. Professor Marc Herold has studied domestic and foreign press reports and calculated more than 3,700 deaths from our bombings.[3]

Also, you have to think about the huge numbers of people, perhaps more than 1 million, who have fled the cities and towns where they live because of the bombing. One refugee camp near Herat, called the "slaughter-house" (*Maslakh*), "is home to more than 350,000 displaced Afghans, of whom 100 die each day of exposure and starvation," the *Guardian* reported in January 2002. The camp is "on the brink of an Ethiopian-style humanitarian disaster."[4]

The flow of refugees started as soon as Bush promised to bomb. There are certain American promises that you can count on, and that's one of them. So, you see the pictures of these families with as many of their possessions as they can carry on their backs and wagons, trying to cross the border. We are terrorizing Afghanistan. The people who live in Kabul and other cities in Afghanistan have to live with the fear of these bombs. Have you lived under bombs? Can you imagine what it's like when you're in a very technologically undeveloped country, and these monster machines are coming over with this ferocious noise, causing these horrible explosions?

It's not right to respond to terrorism by terrorizing other people. And furthermore, it's not going to help. Then you might say, "Yes, it's terrorizing people, but it's worth doing because it will end terrorism." But how much common sense does it take to know that you cannot end terrorism by indiscriminately dropping bombs on Afghanistan? "We have now destroyed several of al-Qaeda's training camps." Who are they kidding? How many hours does it take to set up a training camp? How easy is it to move from one place to another?

George Bush has said that the United States is a target because terrorists oppose our freedoms and democracy. Is that really an explanation of why there is so much animosity against the United States?

Well, it's a useful way to explain what is happening if you want to get public support for the war—to say that it's simple, they don't like our freedom, and they don't like our democracy. Actually, I think there are many people in the Middle East who would like more democracy and more liberty. It seems clear from their own statements that what bothers the people who want to strike at the United States is not what we do internally and how much freedom we have, but what we do externally. What angers them are the troops we've stationed in Saudi Arabia, the enormous economic and military support we give Israel, our maintenance of sanctions against Iraq, which have devastated the country and hurt so many people. They have made it very clear what troubles them.

These issues come up again and again. The journalist Robert Fisk interviewed Osama bin Laden twice for the *Independent* in London. And even while bin Laden invokes religious symbolism and Islam, it is clear from these interviews that bin Laden is infuriated over the military presence of U.S. troops in Saudi Arabia and our policies in Israel and Iraq.[5]

I think there is a simple test of what concerns bin Laden, whether it is our democracy and internal freedom or whether it's our foreign policy. And that simple test is: What side was Osama bin Laden on before 1990? That is, before the United States stationed troops in Saudi Arabia, made war against Iraq, and began its sanctions against Iraq. We were just as democratic and libertarian internally before 1990 as we are today. But Osama bin Laden was not offended by that. He was on our side—and we were on his side—in the fight to take control of the government in Afghanistan. The turning point for Osama bin Laden is very clear. It has nothing to do with democracy and liberty. It has to do with U.S. foreign policy. And that turning point comes in 1990 and 1991.

***Why does the United States have such an interest in
Iraq and such a massive presence in the Middle East?***

Well, I don't think it's hard to figure out why the United
States is so concerned with the Middle East. You can
answer that question with one word: oil. At the time of
World War II, the U.S. government made the decision
that it was going to be the major power controlling the oil
resources of the Middle East. England and France were
the major powers in the Middle East before the war. The
Middle East had been a colonial territory back to the
nineteenth century. But after the war, the old colonial
nations, England and France, were severely weakened,
and the United States emerged as the leading power in
the world. In the middle of World War II, Franklin D.
Roosevelt met with King Ibn Saud of Saudi Arabia and
made arrangements for U.S. corporations to play a role in
Saudi Arabia.

You can trace everything that the United States has
done in the Middle East to the concern for oil—and the
profits from oil. In their candid moments, members of
the U.S. government will affirm that this is their real
concern. And in their more candid moments, commen-
tators who normally support American policy will
admit the same thing. I remember that, before the Gulf
War, the *New York Times* columnist Thomas Friedman
wrote,

> The United States has not sent troops to the Saudi desert to preserve democratic principles. The Saudi monarchy is a feudal regime that does not even allow women to drive cars. Surely it is not American policy to make the world safe for feudalism. This is about money, about protecting governments loyal to America and punishing those that are not and about who will set the price of oil…. Oil is the single most important commodity in the industrial world, and its assured supply at reasonable prices is considered essential for economic growth—not just in the United States but also in Western Europe, Japan and the world at large.[6]

So, the United States has followed this policy of keeping a very close relationship with Israel, on the one hand, and with the oil-producing states, on the other—playing them off against one another so that the United States can be the dominating force in the Middle East.

Can we learn anything from September 11?

We have to think about this awful thing that happened on September 11. We need to feel deeply for the victims and the families. But we also need to learn from it. We have to go beyond grief, anger, and fear to learn something from it. One of the things we need to learn is to begin to see what people are enduring, and have endured, in every part of the world. To see that as clearly and vividly and with as much emotional reaction as we had when we saw these pictures on television from the Twin Towers.

We have to broaden our definition of terrorism, or else we will denounce one terrorism and accept another. And we need to create conditions in the world where the terrorism of sects and the terrorism of governments are both opposed by people all over the world. Terrorism is an international phenomenon. American citizens are not the only victims of terrorism. You hear journalists and politicians talking about globalization and the free flow of markets. But they don't talk about international solidarity of people. They don't say that we should consider people everywhere as our brothers and sisters—that we should consider children all over the world as our children.

To try to explain and understand terrorism is not to justify terrorism. But if you don't try to explain anything, you will never learn anything. We have to dig down and see if we can figure out what is at the root of this horrible act because there's something at the root besides irrational murderous feeling. Yes, September 11 was motivated by a murderous fanatical feeling, but the people who carried out this attack were not simple madmen, like people who go berserk and kill everyone in sight. Terrorism is not that sort of thing.

There's something underneath this fanaticism. There is something in the core belief of these terrorists that may also be at the core belief of millions of other people in the world who are not terrorists, but who are angry at U.S. policy. People who are not fanatic enough to go and kill Americans because they are angry at our policy, but who are capable of doing that if we begin to do even more things to anger them. You might say that there is a reservoir of possible terrorists among all those people in the world who have suffered as a result of U.S. foreign policy. That should concern us.

We have to think about our policies, and ask what we should do to change the image of the United States in the Middle East—and so many other parts of the world. The image of the United States is not that of a peaceful nation. We have our troops everywhere in the world. We have major military bases all over the world. We have naval vessels in every sea in the world. We have to think about what we can do to reshape the image of the United States, not just for the purposes of having a different image. This is not public relations—let's change our image but not the reality. No, we have to change the reality of our policies.

There are things we can do right away to start the process. Remove the troops from Saudi Arabia, which is a very particular grievance for people in the Middle East, not just Osama bin Laden. People there resent that the United States has a military presence near Mecca and Medina. Stop the sanctions that are causing so much suffering in Iraq. And also be very firm and clear with Israel. The U.S. government has to use the power that it has so far used to arm Israel—and, of course, to arm the Arab states, as well; we arm everybody—to bring about a change in its treatment of the Palestinians.

We have to go through a real revolution in our thinking and no longer think of the United States as needing to be a superpower. Sweden is not worried about terrorists. Denmark, Holland, New Zealand. There are a lot of places in the world not worried about terrorists. They don't have their troops everywhere; they don't have their naval vessels everywhere; they're not bothering other people; they're not intervening. They don't have a record of massive military destruction and intervention. Let's be a more modest nation.

If we decide to do that, then all sorts of possibilities open up. Imagine what that $350 billion that we spend every year on being a military superpower could do to help people, to combat AIDS, to feed people, to immunize people. We could use the great wealth that would be freed up by no longer being a military power to pay for free health care for all, affordable housing for all, and helping people in other parts of the world.

A recent report by the World Health Organization calculated that for $101 billion a year in basic medical research and treatment, 8 million lives could be saved annually in the poorer countries of the world.[7] Spending that money on basic health would help in making us more secure. Bombing is not making us more secure.

In the wake of September 11, the Pentagon asked for and received a massive increase in military spending, and Bush has received approval to cut taxes for corpo-

rations and the rich even further. What will be the impact of this on social spending?

It's very interesting that whatever criticism the Democratic Party had of the Bush administration, whatever small amendments they made to the administration's tax bill, and they were always small, there was no really bold, clear Democratic program for taking care of people's needs. And whatever minimal program there once was has now disappeared.

Here is a government that claims to be concerned with human rights and human needs, but it's not concerned with them abroad and it's not concerned with them at home. Historically, of course, this is what happens. I remember during the Vietnam War, the playwright Arthur Miller was invited to the White House by President Johnson. He refused to go, and instead he sent a cable that said, "When the guns boom, the arts die."[8] Not only the arts die, people die. Not just people abroad, but people in this country. The infant mortality rate in the United States is one of the worst among advanced industrial countries, and now it's likely to increase.

The usual situation that existed before this war, of wealth being concentrated at the top while the needs of tens of millions of people in this country are unmet, will become more extreme as a result of war. Already, according to the economist Edward Wolff, the top 1 percent of the wealthy control 38 percent of household wealth. "If we focus more narrowly, on financial wealth," he points out, "the richest 1 percent of households owned 47 percent of the total" in 1998, the last year for which the figures are available. That's a seventy-year high, and the tax cuts, combined with the recession and increased military spending, will increase inequality even further.[9]

In Massachusetts, Governor Jane Swift has called for cutting $20 million from affordable housing programs and $30 million from a program that provides basic dental care to 500,000 poor adult and elderly people in the state.[10]

World War II has come up many times recently, particularly analogies to Pearl Harbor.

History is abused when you create an analogy that will immediately put people on your side without thinking about it carefully. You say, "September 11 is like Pearl Harbor. Since we went to war over Pearl Harbor, now we've got to go to war." Well, is this really like Pearl Harbor? Is there an identifiable nation out there that has attacked us, and that, if attacked in response, will therefore stop attacking us? Is there a nation out there that is expanding its power like Hitler expanding his power in Europe? That's not this situation now. This is a specific and unique situation, and it has to be discussed in its specificity.

The war in Afghanistan is not the first time the United

*States has responded militarily to terrorism. What has
been the result in the past?*

When the U.S. embassies were bombed in Kenya and
Tanzania, immediately Clinton, the liberal president,
sent planes to bomb the Sudan and Afghanistan—because
you've got to bomb somewhere. Clinton said that he had
bombed a facility in Sudan that produced nerve gas. But
it turned out to be an utter lie. It turned out to be a plant
that produced medicines for half the population of the
Sudan.[11] We don't know how many deaths resulted from
bombing that factory.

Sandy Berger, one of Clinton's advisers, went on television at the time of the bombing in Sudan and said the plant
produced chemical weapons. Just recently, Berger was
interviewed on the PBS television program *Frontline*, one
of the few programs on television that occasionally gives
you a different view of things. *Frontline* noted that the
administration at that time said they had bombed a chemical weapons factory, though it actually was a pharmaceu-
tical factory. Berger said, "I think there may have been
some individuals who said the camp was producing [chem-
ical weapons]."[12] And then *Frontline* showed a clip of an
official speaking to a press conference, saying exactly that.
It was Sandy Berger.

That bombing of Afghanistan and the Sudan obviously had no effect on the terrorist act that took place on
September 11, except perhaps to provoke it.

You wrote in an essay called "Just and Unjust War" that "there is no such thing as a just war."[13] How did you reach that conclusion? You didn't start out thinking that.

No, I came to that conclusion as a result of my experience in World War II. Not in the midst of my experience, but afterward, contemplating what was, in terms of just war theory, the closest you could come to a just war. The prospect of fascism dominating the world was absolutely frightful. The war had all of the elements of a just war and overwhelming popular support, from right to left. Not everybody on the left—not the Socialist Workers Party, some of whose members were imprisoned for opposing the war—but certainly the dominant left, the Communist Party left and the liberal left, supported the war.

So if I could begin to feel that this war could not be considered a just war, then the case against war was a serious one. I came to the conclusion that we had reached a point in human history when there probably was no longer a possibility of waging a just war, because the overwhelming technology of modern warfare inevitably involves the killing of large numbers of people. The means overwhelmed any end you could come up with, however important it looked at the moment. Overthrowing a tyrant, preventing aggression, whatever end you could come up with was offset by the horror of the means.

Then you have to consider this: In war, the evil of the means is certain and the achievement of the end, however important, is always uncertain. That is, war always sets off a chain of events that are unpredictable. For instance, in World War II, you could not be certain that you would defeat fascism. You might be fairly certain that you could defeat Hitler and Mussolini; but you could not be certain that you would be doing away with all the elements of fascism, with militarism, racism, imperialism, and violence. In fact, after 50 million deaths, that did not happen. Considering those issues, and thinking about the prospects for the human race given the horrific technology of war, persuaded me that there could no longer really be a war that we could call just. I decided that whatever problems we faced, whatever tyranny we faced, whatever world situation we faced, whatever act of aggression we faced, we had to come up with a solution other than the mass killing of human beings.

And, sure, that leaves you with a problem. The question always comes up about World War II: "What would you have done?" The answer is not an easy one, but it has to start off by saying, "I would not accept a solution that involves mass killing. I would try to find some other way." The other way is not passivity; the other way is not acceptance; the other way is resistance without war. The other way is underground movements, strikes, general strikes, noncompliance. Even Hitler, in World War II, was at times successfully resisted in Denmark, in Norway, in Germany itself, by wives protesting the deportation of their Jewish husbands. Those methods of resistance don't ensure a peaceful resolution, because the repressive forces are always strong. But they are means that are more proportional to the end, especially since they are means that are engaged in not by governments but by people, which is a very important consideration. With popular resistance, you have a greater assurance that your end will be attained than if governments are in charge.

Take the war that was presumably fought to save the people in Kosovo from Slobodan Milosevic. Again, one can identify a moral element to that. But what did the United States and NATO do in the course of the war? They created more havoc, more refugees, more dead than there were before. They bombed Yugoslavia and killed civilians. Because war is inevitably indiscriminate, innocent people are killed. In fact, the politicians admit it. They say, "Well, yes, innocent people will be killed, but it is too bad." This is what terrorists say. That's what Timothy McVeigh said.

When Timothy McVeigh was asked about the kids who were killed in the Oklahoma City bombing, he said that they were "collateral damage."[14] He used the same language that the U.S. government used in the Gulf War, of which he was a veteran. But that collateral damage is human beings dying. The people who died in New York are collateral damage to the terrorists, and the people who were dying in the bombings in Afghanistan are collateral damage to our government.

The term "just war" contains an internal contradic-

Howard Zinn

tion. War is inherently unjust, and the great challenge of our time is to how to deal with evil, tyranny, and oppression without killing huge numbers of people.

Would you describe yourself as a pacifist?

I have never used the word "pacifist" to describe myself because it suggests something absolute, and I am suspicious of absolutes. I think there might be situations when a small, focused act of violence against a monstrous evil would be justified. Even such committed pacifists as Gandhi and Martin Luther King believed this.

The question of pacifism is interesting. Scott Simon of National Public Radio wrote a commentary in the *Wall Street Journal* on October 11 titled "Even Pacifists Must Support This War." Simon, who is a Quaker, wrote that "American pacifists have no sane alternative now but to support war." He tried to use the pacifist acceptance of self-defense, which approves a focused resistance to an immediate attacker, to justify this war. But the term "self-defense" does not apply when you drop bombs in heavily populated residential areas and kill people other than your attacker. And it doesn't apply when there is no likelihood that this action will make the world less violent.[15]

How do we evaluate terrorism when it's undertaken by people who are resisting direct oppression, such as military occupation or dispossession?

I don't think that terrorism is justified even though the end is a just one. The demands of the Palestinians are just, but I don't think terrorist acts are justified, on both moral and pragmatic grounds. First, I don't think it's justified to set off a bomb in a marketplace or discotheque and kill innocent people, even if the cause is just. Second, from a pragmatic point of view, terrorism inevitably calls upon itself—or, rather, the people it purports to represent—counterterrorism. We've seen this in Israel and in Palestine. We have seen car bombs met by massive Israeli force; the cycle has gone on for years and years.

I remember talking to Eqbal Ahmad, who during his lifetime was one of the most astute observers of guerrilla movements and third-world struggles, and one of the wisest people around. He spoke out very forcefully against terrorism. There is a wonderful discussion of terrorism in his book of interviews with David Barsamian in which he says, "You do not solve social problems by individual acts of violence. Social problems require social and political mobilization."[16]

2

SEARCHING FOR COMMON GROUND

The proponents of the war in Afghanistan say it has made the world a safer place. It seems like the war is actually going to make it a more dangerous one.

Bush has to insist that the war has made the world a safer place. Otherwise there is no rationale for the havoc we have wreaked on Afghanistan. The havoc has been minimized and obscured by both the government and the press, but I think there is very little doubt that we have not made the world a safer place.

On December 20, 2001, the *New York Times* acknowledged that after all of this destruction, "Virtually the entire top leadership of the Taliban has survived the American bombing and eluded capture by American-backed Afghan forces."[17]

They say, "We are going to do away with terrorism," but there is no indication that they have. The Bush administration has itself said that al-Qaeda has cells in many countries. Then they say they are after bin Laden, and he becomes the focus; but they can't find bin Laden. And then they say they want the Taliban leaders; yet now they can't get the Taliban leaders. So, even from their own stated objectives—getting the Taliban's leaders or al-Qaeda or bin Laden—they have failed.

I think we also have to say that these objectives are dubious, because even if they were achieved, the likely outcome is not the end of terrorism. So, from their own point of view, their own objectives, they fail. And from the standpoint of a person concerned with human needs rather than power politics, what has happened in Afghanistan is an atrocity.

Then we have to point out the immediate danger that the United States, having run out of targets in Afghanistan, is considering military action against Iraq. People in the Bush administration are also talking about waging wars in other countries like Somalia and Syria. I notice they don't mention Turkey or Saudi Arabia. There is a precise division between who we bomb and who we don't bomb. The division has nothing to do with which countries may be harboring terrorists. The division has only to do with which countries we don't control yet. The countries that we control, like Turkey and Saudi Arabia, can harbor as many terrorists as they want. We will look elsewhere.

The advantage of this strategy of expanding the war and winning the "war on terrorism" is that it gives the government a perpetual war and a perpetual atmosphere of repression. And it generates perpetual profits for corporations. But it's going to make the world a far more unstable and dangerous place.

If the United States extends the war in Afghanistan into Iraq, it will have a disastrous effect on American relations with the Arab world and with Muslims. Because then it will be understood that the United States is not confining its violence to Afghanistan. All the disclaimers of Bush that we have nothing against Islam will disintegrate if we attack other countries. And we will be attacking other countries with the same lack of discrimination and horrific human results we have seen in Afghanistan.

I think the American public has not yet absorbed the statements that the Bush administration is making about this being a war that will go on and on. People need to ask, "Do we want our children and our grandchildren to be living in a state of perpetual warfare, with more and more of the world becoming hostile to us, and with the United States responsible for more and more human casualties in the world?"

The antiwar movement has been weak during this war. The number of voices speaking out against the war has been quite small.

One problem is that we don't have a national antiwar movement, like we did during the Vietnam War and to some extent during the Gulf War. So what we have is a kind of decentralized antiwar movement. The fact that it is decentralized, and that there is no one national focus, means that hundreds and hundreds of antiwar actions have taken place around the country but received little attention.

I don't know what the total number of actions has been. I can only judge from the fact that everywhere I go in the country—and I've done a lot of traveling since September 11 and since the bombing of Afghanistan began—a substantial number of people oppose the war.

I just received an e-mail from Missoula, Montana, about an antiwar parade there. "About 100 people marched through downtown Missoula...calling for peaceful alternatives to the military strikes," the Associated Press reported.[18] I figure if there is an antiwar parade in Missoula, then there must be an antiwar sentiment in every state of the union, in every town and city.

The press has done a terrible job of reporting about antiwar sentiment. This creates a greater responsibility for people on the left to get information out about what people around the country are doing and saying. I just got another e-mail about an antiwar demonstration at Rockefeller Center.[19] You know what Rockefeller Center is like before Christmas. It's wild with holiday spirit and decorations—and, now, flags and so on—but people were handing out leaflets and making speeches against the war. Apparently the onlookers were very kind, and the protesters heard expressions of support from people who were passing by.

What has been the impact of people like Richard Falk, who has been an opponent of so many U.S. military interventions, calling the war in Afghanistan a "just war"?

I'm sure that Richard Falk's uncertainty about the war—and I call it uncertainty because he has gone back and forth several times about the war—is shared by a number of people on the left.[20] It is certainly shared by the editors of *The Nation* magazine, which has printed his articles on the war.

I think that people who talk about a limited military response either don't know, or have forgotten, that military action does not have built-in limits. The natural tendency of military action is to go as far as it can, using everything in its destructive arsenal. As we have seen since World War II, military action has been extended just short of nuclear war, with the government even coming close to considering it on some occasions. And in World War II, we did use nuclear weapons.

I also think intimidation has been a factor. You don't like to think that people on the left are intimidated, but all of us are subject to that. When you are surrounded by television reports supporting the war and flags waving, it has an effect.

I also think that some people on the left have been intimidated by the statistic that 90 percent of the public supports the war. What the left often does in what I

would consider its weaker moments is to try to ingrati-
ate itself with the majority of the population. There are
understandable grounds for this: we shouldn't be sectari-
an and isolate ourselves. The principle here is legitimate.
I think it's right to say, "Let's see where the majority of
the population is, even if we think that this majority is
wrong. Let's see where the majority is and let's see in
what way we can find common ground with people." But
I think that common ground should not rest on an
acceptance of something we believe to be wrong. There
are ways of reaching common ground with that 90 percent that do not involve supporting the bombing of
Afghanistan.

We can find common ground in what I believe is a
universal instinct for compassion. We can present to the
American public the information that they're not getting about the human effects of our bombing. We can
put out front what has been on the back pages of the
New York Times—the very specific, chilling accounts
from reporters on the spot in villages, and in hospitals,
of children who have lost arms and legs and eyes, of
people who have been really seriously injured, of villagers who are burying thirty and forty people. If we
share such graphic accounts of the human toll of this
war with the American people, they cannot help but be
moved by that. After all, they were moved by what happened to the people in New York because they saw it up
front.

The problem with the casualties in Afghanistan is that they have not been presented in as graphic a way as the human suffering caused by the attack on the Twin Towers. People are dying because they happen to live in Afghanistan in villages in the vicinity of vaguely defined "military targets." This is itself a form of terrorism, but it isn't graphically shown to us.

The victims of our bombing in Afghanistan have not been humanized in the same way as the *New York Times* has humanized the victims of September 11 in the daily "Portraits in Grief" section of the paper. Every day, for several months, the *Times* has been doing what should always be done when a tragedy is summed up in a statistic: it has printed miniature portraits of the human beings who died in the attacks of September 11—their names, photographs, what they enjoyed, their idiosyncrasies, how loved ones remembered them. The director of the New York Historical Society, Kenneth Jackson, said about this recurring page in the *Times*,

> The peculiar genius of it was to put a human face on numbers that are unimaginable to most of us.... As you read those individual portraits about love affairs or kissing children goodbye or coaching soccer and buying a dream house...it's so obvious that every one of them was a person who deserved to live a full and successful and happy life. You see what was lost.[21]

I was deeply moved when I read these sketches—"A Poet of Bensonhurst," "Someone to Lean On," "A Friend, A Sister," "Laughter, Win Or Lose."[22] What if, instead of seeing these people as symbols, those who celebrated the grisly deaths of the people in the Twin Towers and the Pentagon as a blow to symbols of American dominance in the world could see, up close, the faces of those who lost their lives? I wonder if they would have second thoughts, second feelings.

And what if all those people who declare their support for Bush's "war on terrorism" could see the real human beings who are dying under our bombs, not just the media images of al-Qaeda or Osama bin Laden? What if they learned more about the many human tragedies in Afghanistan—the names of the dead, images of the villages that were bombed, the words of a father who lost his children, the ages of the children? I think they would have second thoughts. Unlike the fanatics in Washington and around the country who are willing—like their counterparts around the world—to kill for some cause, most Americans would begin to understand that the war we are waging is a war on ordinary men, women, and children, especially if the stories of people in Afghanistan were told.

I also think that there is a common ground if we make clear that our objective is the same: to do away with terrorism. We need to make a clear distinction of accepting this as an objective, while challenging the means and the claim of the administration that bombing Afghanistan is going to end terrorism. Once you say to people, "Yes, we must do away with terrorism. But let's think intelligently about how we do it. Let's not react simply with anger," I think we can find common ground.

Another possible common ground is to point to the families of some of the survivors and some of the victims of the Twin Towers tragedy, those families that have come forth and said: "We do not want revenge." The *Wall Street Journal* had an interesting headline on October 8: "Many Relatives of Victims Feel Uneasy, Fear Innocent Will Die in Retaliation." The article quoted Charles Christophe, whose wife died on September 11, saying, "If I could, I would like to prevent the death[s] of more innocent people." Orlando and Phyllis Rodriguez lost their thirty-one-year-old son on September 11. "Nothing will erase the pain and loss that we must learn to live with, and causing others pain can only make it worse," they wrote.[23]

I think most people have supported this war because they hope it will in some way be effective in stopping terrorism. But I think they would be repelled by the idea that revenge is driving our policy.

I just heard from a man I met in Greensboro, North Carolina, a writer named David Potorti, whose brother was killed in the Twin Towers. He took part in a march from Washington, D.C., to New York City of the families of victims of September 11. The marchers wanted to express their strong feelings about moving away from revenge and looking for more humane solutions to the problem of terrorism. The *New York Times* showed a photograph of David and other people from the march on December 2, 2001, but the caption did not explain that they were protesting the war. David wrote a letter to the *Times*, explaining,

> While the *Times* was accurate in depicting our presence at a "vigil," it did not show the signs we carried, or mention that the vigil was the culmination of an eight-day walk for healing and peace…. Our motive, and that of our fellow marchers, was to seek alternatives to war as a response to our personal and national tragedies. While your photographer did a great job, we did not come to New York to get our picture taken. We came to demand an end to the war in Afghanistan.

But the *Times* didn't run his letter, only printing a correction that the caption "described the event incompletely" by not mentioning that it "marked the end of an eight-day peace march."[24]

Global Exchange in San Francisco helped organize a visit of family members of people who died on September 11 to Afghanistan. The trip brought together people who lost loved ones in the attacks with people in Afghanistan who lost family to the U.S. bombing. Rita Lasar, whose brother died in the World Trade Center, met a man

Howard Zinn

named Amin Said, whose brother was killed two months later in Kabul because of a "wayward bomb." He said to her, "He was your brother, but he was also my brother. We are all brothers and sisters."[25]

Another very important issue is that the war has obscured the fact that many people in this country are still in need. There have just been some reports on the number of people in this country who are hungry, the children who are undernourished. The *New York Times* reported that "with unemployment rising and housing costs still high, cities around the country are experiencing a new and sudden wave of homelessness. Shelters are overflowing, and more people this year are sleeping on floors in dingy social service centers, living in cars or spending nights on the streets."[26] The five-year limit set by the Democratic and Republican legislation ending the federal guarantee for Aid for Families with Dependent Children is coming to an end. All of this is being obscured by the war.

We need to dig under the rubble of war and point out that the Bush administration is using the war as a cover for worsening the income gap in this country, while paying no attention to the problems of most of the American people, while enriching corporations. I think concentrating on the class issue, concentrating on the benefits being given to corporations, is critical. Look at the current so-called economic stimulus package. I always choke on that word "stimulus." Whom are they stimulating? It's very stimulating to General Motors, and it's very depressing to the rest of the country to see IBM, GM, and Ford getting $70 billion in tax breaks.[27]

I think that the issue of economic justice is something that people immediately respond to. I was just talking on the telephone with Seymour Melman of Columbia University, who has just written a remarkably optimistic book called *After Capitalism*.[28] He made an important point about the tactics of the antiwar movement. He said that the left is in a position of continually opposing war after war after war, without getting at the root of the problem—which is the economic system under which we live, which needs war and makes war inevitable. His point is that it's really an uphill struggle to concentrate on war in an atmosphere of such intense patriotism, whereas a greater concentration on economic issues—not neglecting the war, of course—and on the failure of this system to take care of human needs would give us a much stronger bond with the American people. In fact, it would make them more likely to listen to what we have to say about the war.

Do you think the attack on civil liberties that is a consequence of this war is another area for forging common ground?

Definitely. This is an important area for common ground, though the issue of civil liberties is tricky because the polls do show that many people seem to be willing to restrict liberties on the ground that this is necessary to carry on the war. I think their willingness to accept these restrictions is based on the idea that it will somehow help find the perpetrators of terrorism. So, challenging this idea requires a double argument, one in which you point out that the war is not going to really solve the problem of terrorism and a second one in which you show that these new restrictions are going to endanger the liberties of all of us.

It's not only Muslims who will be affected. I think we ought to circulate wherever we can Pastor Niemöller's famous statement about the Nazis because it's so applicable to the present situation:

> First they came for the Communists, but I was not a Communist—so I said nothing. Then they came for the Social Democrats, but I was not a Social Democrat—so I did nothing. Then came the trade unionists, but I was not a trade unionist. And then they came for the Jews, but I was not a Jew—so I did little. Then when they came for me, there was no one left who could stand up for me.[29]

It's not just Muslims who are in danger but anyone who speaks out. There are about 20 million immigrants, short-term guests, and noncitizens in this country. Now, by executive order and because Congress passed the USA PATRIOT Act, all are potentially subject to military trials, expedited deportations, and indefinite detention. As Anthony Lewis put it, millions of people "who came here to struggle for a better life will now know that they are at risk of being detained and tried by a military tribunal if someone thinks they have something to do with terrorism."[30]

According to the *New York Times*, Congress has also "given the CIA new legal powers to snoop on people in the United States," overturning the restrictions placed on the agency in the 1970s after people exposed its abuses of civil liberties. Supreme Court Justice Sandra Day O'Connor said after visiting "ground zero" in New York, "We're likely to experience more restrictions on our personal freedom than has ever been the case in our country." When a Supreme Court justice says that, it should be a real concern to all of us.[31]

According to Nancy Chang, an attorney at the Center for Constitutional Rights, the Bush administration's actions since September 11 "portend a wholesale suspension of civil liberties that will reach far beyond those who are involved in terrorist activities." She says that a possible outcome of the USA PATRIOT Act is "the criminalization of legitimate political dissent" and warns that it "grants the executive branch unprecedented, and largely unchecked, surveillance powers, including the enhanced ability to track email and Internet usage, conduct sneak-and-peak searches, obtain sensitive personal records, [and] monitor financial transactions."[32]

Antiwar sentiment seems much stronger abroad, but this opposition has been dismissed as "anti-Americanism" in the media.

I think the reason antiwar sentiment is weaker in the United States than abroad has a lot to do with the fact that the attack took place here and had a very traumatic effect on people in this country. It has been very difficult for an antiwar movement to deal with this trauma, to get through it, and to ask important questions about our policies.

People who are not in the United States often have a broader perspective. Many of them have endured acts of terrorism and other traumatic events, some of them even more horrific than September 11. So, I think they are able to take a larger view of this. I recently received an e-mail from a man in Bombay. He talked about natural disasters and disasters caused by corporations, like the deadly Bhopal gas leak, which caused much greater loss of life than took place at the Twin Towers. These tragedies have not brought signs of mourning in the United States, whereas we have had endless manifestations of mourning related to September 11. Not that this mourning for the victims of the Twin Towers is misplaced. Yes, we should mourn. But why can't we also mourn for people in other countries who have been victims of deliberate human profiteering and war?

This whole question of "anti-Americanism" needs to be dissected. I think that if you look closely at the way people abroad react to America, you will see a very ambivalent reaction. On one hand, you see intense hostility toward American policies, American corporate domination, and certainly American military interventions abroad. On the other hand, you see again and again that individual Americans, American people, are looked upon in a very friendly way.

I have a friend who is working in the Peace Corps in Morocco. She is an American Jew living in Morocco, a Muslim country, and she writes to me about how friendly people are to her, even as they demonstrate in the streets against American policies.

With the current recession, it looks like the war in Afghanistan also raises a number of "guns versus butter" issues.

I don't think the American people have been informed about how much money is being spent on the war. Most people in general have a very vague idea about what the military budget consists of and how large it is. Even a portion of the U.S. military budget could solve fundamental problems of health and security for large numbers of Americans. That's an important issue to talk about.

Take the National Missile Defense program. That's immediately $8.3 billion right there. *The Economist* magazine reported that the cost of a "fully deployed system" could cost closer to $200 billion.[33]

The Bush administration is now asking for a $48 billion increase in military spending, the largest hike since Ronald Reagan's first year in office. "On top of all this," the *New York Times* reported, "the Pentagon is planning to ask Congress within the next two months for an emergency budget supplement to pay for the current costs of the war in Afghanistan. Congress appropriated $17.5 billion for that purpose late last year."[34]

That money, coupled with Bush's $1.3 trillion tax cut, is going to be taken away from social programs that are already underfunded. Bush's new military budget "will make the vise all the tighter for everything else," the *Wall Street Journal* reported recently. It's going to come from mental health programs, education, health care, prescription drugs for the elderly, and public housing. The *New York Times* had a headline on January 14 that said "Grim Choices Face States in Making Cuts in Medicaid." These cuts are going to affect millions of people.[35]

And it's not just a matter of guns versus butter in this country; it's a matter of guns versus human rights worldwide. The *Financial Times* recently noted that the U.S. government spends only 0.1 percent of its national income on foreign aid. And not all of that foreign aid is humanitarian.[36]

You read about the pitiful sum that the United States is willing to expend on the massive global problem of AIDS. The United States contributes only $460 million a year to international efforts to combat AIDS, when billions are needed. The United States could spare those billions of dollars and save millions of lives if it weren't spending all of that money on the military.[37]

I think that people will understand that not only is there an immediate humanitarian effect of spending this money to do something about AIDS, but from a long-term point of view the security of the people of the United States depends on the health and well-being of the rest of the world.

Bush has been getting a free ride in the media during the war. The New York Times wrote an appalling editorial called "Mr. Bush's New Gravitas" in which they said he "was in full command of the complex array of political and military challenges that he faces."[38]

It's not just the *New York Times*. There are people on the left who have said admiring things about Bush, that he has done a good job so far in the war. Many of them were deceived—really a surprising naivete from supposedly sophisticated observers—by Bush's early statements promising a cautious and limited response to the events of September 11.

To me, those liberals, even radicals, who have to some degree supported the war have made a pact with the devil, which they themselves do not understand. They consoled themselves with phrases like "limited military action" and "measured response," as if there was something measured or limited about cluster bombs, fifteen-thousand-pound Daisy Cutters, and carpet bombing. They think they can separate the war from all of its other consequences. They think they can say on the one hand, "Well, we may have to carry out a limited military action," and on the other hand decry the attacks on civil liberties.

You see this again and again in the liberal press. They support the war, and yet they think that Attorney General John Ashcroft ordering the detention of people and secret evidence hearings is wrong. They don't seem to understand that you can't have one without the other. That's the devil's pact liberals and people on the left have signed and that they don't want to acknowledge.

Christopher Hitchens has been particularly vituperative in his attacks on people who have spoken out against the war.

People like Hitchens are distorting seriously the position of people who are against this war. They impute to people like me and Noam Chomsky ideas that we do not express, and claim falsely that we are justifying what happened in New York or that we are saying, "We deserved it." None of the people I know who have spoken out against the war have said anything like that.

You were named on a list of people expressing "blame America first" ideas. It was published by Lynne Cheney and the American Council of Trustees and Alumni (ACTA). The first draft of the report, later changed, said professors were "the weak link in America's response to the attack."[39]

Yes. I was happy to be on the list. I remember my disappointment of not being on President Nixon's enemies list and being overlooked on a lot of these lists. Of course, the FBI has not overlooked me. They had a huge file on me. But there were times when I felt neglected....

Drawing up a list of people who have made statements against the war, and implying that these are people beyond the pale, fits in with the statements John Ashcroft has made about people who oppose his repressive policies. In testimony before the Senate Judiciary Committee on December 6, he said, "[T]o those who scare peace-loving people with phantoms of lost liberty, my message is this: Your tactics only aid terrorists, for they erode our national unity and diminish our resolve. They give ammunition to America's enemies, and pause to America's friends."[40] That's almost straight out of the constitutional definition of treason, which is punishable by death.

If you look at them, the statements quoted on ACTA's list are the most innocuous statements. Jesse Jackson made the list by saying that America should "build bridges and relationships, not simply bombs and walls." And I was criticized for saying that "our security can only come by using our national wealth not for guns, planes, and bombs, but for the health and welfare of our people, and for people suffering in other countries."[41] The simple exercise of the First Amendment, of saying that we should be able to criticize our government, is enough to put you on Lynne Cheney's list. I think that should be brought to more people's attention because I think Americans are sensitive to invasions of free speech. Unfortunately, they are most aroused when it's directed at American citizens rather than only at Muslims or immigrants.

This time reminds me very much of the Cold War period. During the Cold War period, people in power were blacklisting not only members of Communist organizations but a much wider range of people. They made a distinction between "Communist action" organizations, "Communist front" organizations, and "Communist sympathetic" organizations, but all were considered dangerous.

I remember I was living a good part of that period in Atlanta, Georgia, and in order to continue teaching at Georgia State University, a friend of mine had to sign an oath in which he swore not only that *he* was not a member of a long list of different organizations, including the Yugoslav Seamen's Club and Nature Friends of America, but that no *relative* of his had been a member of these organizations.

This extension of the search for troublemakers is very reminiscent of the kind of absurdities we saw in the 1950s. The McCarran-Walter Immigration Act in 1952 created the legal basis for deportations without trial, which the Bush administration is now reviving. The Internal Security Act of 1950 authorized the actual setting up of concentration camps that would be used to incarcerate people who were threats to national security. Recall that Martin Luther King Jr. was seen as a threat to national security by the FBI and put on their "Reserve Index" of people who were "likely to furnish financial and other material aid to subversive associations and ideology." According to historian David Garrow, the list was intended "to make detention of allegedly dangerous individuals as easy as possible in the event of a presidentially declared national emergency. The Atlanta [FBI] office was advised that King should be added to its pick-up list."[42]

There is another important connection between our situation today and the Cold War. Terrorism has replaced Communism as the rationale for the militarization of the country, for military adventures abroad, and for the suppression of civil liberties at home. It serves the same purpose, serving to create hysteria.

The word "communism" was used to justify the most egregious violations of human rights. So much that went on during the Cold War was justified in the name of fighting Communism, leading to the deaths of millions of people in Southeast Asia and hundreds of thousands of people in Central America. A vast leap took place from "fighting Communism" to actions against people and governments that had nothing to do with Communism. In 1954, the

Howard Zinn

United States overthrew the government in Guatemala, which was not Communist but which was expropriating the United Fruit Company. In 1973, the government in Chile was overthrown in the name of fighting Communism. The government was not Communist, but it was not serving the interests of Anaconda Copper and ITT.

We have to bring up this history and relate it to what is happening today. Now that the Cold War is over, I think it's possible for Americans to assess more calmly the things that we did during the Cold War, which now seem obviously absurd, and to suggest that the "war on terrorism" is being used in the same way.

3

A PEACEFUL NATION?

When George Bush announced the bombing of Afghanistan had started, he said, "We are a peaceful nation."[43] *What is your reaction to that?*

Well, obviously Bush hasn't read any history and does not remember any history, even the history of his own time, because the United States has been involved in wars and military actions for a very long time. You can't tell the Native Americans we were a peaceful nation as we moved across the continent and engaged in hundreds of wars against the Indians. The United States engaged in at least twenty military interventions in the Caribbean in the first twenty years of the last century. And then from World War II through today, we've had an endless succession of wars and military interventions.

Just five years after the end of the most disastrous war in world history, after World War II, we are at war in Korea. And then almost immediately we are helping the French in Indochina, supplying 80 percent of their military equipment, and soon we are involved in Southeast Asia. We are bombing not only Vietnam but Cambodia and Laos.

In the 1950s, we are also involved in covert operations, overthrowing the governments of Iran and Guatemala. And almost as soon as we get involved in Vietnam, we are sending military troops into the Dominican Republic. In that period, we are also giving enormous amounts of aid to the government of Indonesia, helping the dictator Suharto carry on an internal war against the opposition, in the course of which several hundred thousand people are killed. Then the U.S. government, starting in 1975, provides critical support to Indonesia's brutal campaign to subdue the people of East Timor, in which hundreds of thousands of people are killed.

In the 1980s, when Reagan comes into office, we begin a covert war throughout Central America, in El Salvador, Honduras, Costa Rica, and especially in Nicaragua, creating the counterrevolutionary force, the Contras, whom Reagan called "freedom fighters."

In 1978, even before the Russians were in Afghanistan, we are covertly sending arms to the rebel forces in Afghanistan, the *mujahedeen*. Some of these people turned out later to be the Taliban, the people who suddenly are our enemy. The national security adviser to Carter, Zbigniew Brzezinski, boasted that he knew U.S. aid would "induce a Soviet military intervention" in Afghanistan. In fact, this happened, provoking a war that lasted ten years.[44] The war was devastating to the people of Afghanistan and left the country in ruins. The moment it was over, the United States immediately moved out. The people that we supported, the fundamentalists, took power in Afghanistan and established their regime.

Almost as soon as George Bush Sr. came into office, in 1989, he launched a war against Panama, which left perhaps several thousand dead. Two years later, we were at war in the Gulf, using the invasion of Kuwait as an excuse to intensify our military presence in that area and to station troops in Saudi Arabia, which then became one of the major offenses for Osama bin Laden and other Saudi Arabian nationalists. Then in the Clinton administration we were bombing Afghanistan, Sudan, Yugoslavia, and Iraq again.

So for Bush to call us "a peaceful nation" means forgetting an enormous amount of history. Now, maybe that history is too much for Bush to take in, but even a small part of it would be enough to suggest that we have not been a peaceful nation. In fact, it is safe to say that since World War II, there has not been a more warlike nation in the world than the United States.

The **New York Times** *had a headline on September 23, 2001, that read "Forget the Past: It's a War Unlike Any Other."*[45] *What would happen if we followed this advice?*

They want us to act as if we were born yesterday. They want us to forget the history of our government. Because if you forget history, if you were born yesterday, then you'll believe anything.

How do you think we got Texas, Colorado, New Mexico, Arizona, and California? Because the Mexicans liked us and gave them to us? No. We acquired that territory in the Mexican War. And we thought the Mexicans should be grateful that we didn't take it all.

But the Mexican War began with a lie. There was an incident on the Mexican border. American troops went into this disputed area and people were killed. President James Polk said that blood had been spilled on American soil, and soon the armies were on their way to Mexico City. Not long after, we had half of Mexico.

In 1898, the battleship *Maine* was sunk in Havana Harbor, which led to the Spanish-American War. By the way, no one ever asked what the *Maine* was doing in Havana Harbor. This was like when the U.S. ship was bombed in Yemen a few years ago. I didn't see reporters ask, "What is an American destroyer doing there?"

If people knew some history, if teachers gave them history, if the media gave people history, if anyone with power over communications networks gave them some history, they might recognize in this rush of Congress to war the same subservience as we have seen in the past. When Bush went to Congress after September 11, everyone there acted as if there were no need to think and to ask questions about what we should do. They voted unanimously in the Senate and almost unanimously in the House of Representatives. There was only one dissenting vote. When I heard that, I thought that dissenting vote must have been Bernie Sanders, the Independent from Vermont, but it wasn't. It was Barbara Lee from California.

So, history can be useful. It can tell you something about government, about lies and deception. If people knew that history, they wouldn't just sit and listen to Bush and be impressed that he knows how to read.

If we don't know that history, we won't understand how much animosity we have engendered elsewhere in the world—not just in the Middle East but all over the world. In its foreign policy, the United States has consigned several million people to their deaths and supported terrorist governments in various parts of the world, especially in Latin America and the Middle East.

If we don't have any history, we'll live our lives believing what we're taught in school, that America is a beacon for democracy and freedom in the world. We'll think that we've been the Boy Scouts of the world, helping countries across the street.

The Uruguayan writer Eduardo Galeano has written about the School of the Americas, now renamed the Western Hemisphere Institute for Security Cooperation. He writes that in the United States, "military nurseries [have] been growing specialists in the violations of human rights."[46] It seems that if the United States was

really interested in shutting down terrorist training camps, it could start much closer to home in Fort Benning, Georgia.

Yes, we live in an age of irony. There was the Stone Age, and now there is the Age of Irony. The government says it is determined to close terrorist camps, yet here in the United States the School of the Americas has trained people who have engaged in terrorism, trained people who then became organizers of death squads in Central America.

If you put up photos of the graduating classes of the School of the Americas on the wall, you would have a rogues' gallery of terrorism. I think of the El Salvadoran death squad leader Roberto D'Aubuisson; of the graduates who took part in the massacre of 811 people in El Mozote in December 1981; of the many generals and dictators who went through the School of the Americas. In fact, some of the manuals used in the School of the Americas give advice on how to carry out what amount to terrorist acts.[47]

You know, the Panamanian dictator Manuel Noriega went to the School of the Americas and then became an employee of the CIA; but then suddenly he becomes an enemy and a terrorist, so we go to war to capture him. But we probably won't go to war to get Kissinger anytime soon. The United States has consistently opposed the creation of an international war crimes tribunal because it could be used against people in the U.S. government and military. They are very explicit about it. In effect, the government is saying, "Yes, we have people who could be accused of having committed war crimes." The United States wants to find other people who have committed war crimes, but an American by definition cannot commit a war crime.

In fact, Kissinger wrote recently that the proposal to create an international court is a bad idea.[48] Well, naturally it's a bad idea, because he would be one of the first people who would be up there on the witness stand trying to explain his support for death squads and repressive governments in Latin America, war crimes in Southeast Asia, and the apartheid South African government.

It would be good to have an international war crimes trial that would be truly evenhanded in bringing up for prosecution people in all countries of the world who have engaged in and supported, or conspired to support, terrorism. But the U.S. government is clearly not interested in that.

4

THE NEED FOR DISSENT

You hear a common refrain now: "We have to line up behind our president."

Phrases such as the one Bush used after September 11— "Either you are with us or you are with the terrorists"— are rather terrifying.[49] It means that if you're not supporting the government, you're an enemy of the government. All of this produces a kind of hysteria, which leads to what I think can only be described as a lynch spirit.

You can see it coming not just from the government but from the major media. Andrew Sullivan, an editor at the *New Republic*, wrote about a "fifth column" being constituted by antiwar activists in the United States.[50] The idea of a fifth column goes back to the Spanish Civil War, referring to people in your midst who are traitors. This is very dangerous talk, and it's very threatening and intimidating to people who now do not feel free to express their opinions for fear of being considered traitors.

To me, this idea that "you mustn't criticize your government and you must fall in line behind the president" is really a great danger to the very democracy that Bush claims we are defending by going to war.

On September 29, Al Gore spoke to the Iowa Democratic Party and received a standing ovation when he said, "George W. Bush is my commander in chief," and, in the words of the *New York Times*, "implored Democrats and Republicans alike to offer Mr. Bush their unwavering support."[51] When I heard that, I thought to myself, I don't think Al Gore has read the Constitution. The Constitution says the president is the commander in chief of the armed forces. He's not the commander in chief of the country, of all of us. Gore is another example of people rushing to get into line, to get inside the perimeter of power.

I think of Dan Rather, the CBS news anchor. What is he anchored to? He's anchored to the establishment. That's what an anchorman is. Rather went on the *Late Show with David Letterman* and said, "George Bush is the president, he makes the decisions, and, you know, as just one American, he wants me to line up, just tell me where." Rather also went on *Larry King Live* and said, "[W]hatever arguments one may or may not have had with George Bush the younger before September Eleventh, he is our commander in chief, he's the man now. And we need unity, we need steadiness. I'm not preaching about it. We all know this."[52]

This is the language you might hear in a totalitarian state, not in a democracy: If the president says get in line, we get in line. The first rule of journalism is to be an independent voice, an independent critic, not a handmaiden of government, to be someone who represents the public and the government and does not immediately say, "Yes, we're together." When we turn on CNN, we shouldn't see the American flag constantly on the screen.

It is also supposed to be part of the American tradition that if we want to step out of line, we step out of line. Democracy isn't falling in line behind the president. Democracy is for people to think independently, be skeptical of government, look around and try to find out what's going on. And if they find out that government is deceiving them, to speak out as loudly as they can. That's democracy.

You recently stirred up some controversy for speaking to Newton North High School students and raising some questions about the U.S. bombing of Afghanistan. The **Boston Herald** *reports that "parents questioned exposing young teens to Zinn's opinions" and quotes a parent, whose children interestingly don't attend the school, saying, "It's unbelievable what this guy did.... It's horrifying. He told these things to an entire school audience of kids 13 to 17 who don't know any better."*[53]

Of course, this *Herald* reporter misrepresented what I said when he said I "equated the U.S. military strikes in Afghanistan with the Sept. 11 terrorist attacks" in the opening paragraph of that article. So that's a good way to start a story, by misquoting a very crucial statement made by the person you are writing about. Equating the U.S. military strikes in Afghanistan with September 11? No, of course I didn't equate the two. I said the U.S. military strikes in Afghanistan were not the appropriate way to respond to terrorism, that using violence against innocent people, against civilians in Afghanistan, is not a moral way to respond to terrorism.

It's possible to compare the two events and say that just as the attack on the World Trade Center was an immoral act of terrorism, the killing of civilians in Afghanistan and the driving of hundreds of thousands of people from their homes in Afghanistan is an immoral act, without trying to equate them. You can't really equate any two atrocities, but you can put them side by side and suggest that they're both evil and that one does not compensate for the other.

As for the parent of these three Newton students who aren't yet in high school, who says it's "unbelievable" what I said, that's interesting. My book *A People's History of the United States* is used in high schools all over the country by kids thirteen to seventeen.[54] And as a parent myself, I wonder about the kind of education he wants for his kids. Does he really think that kids of high school age are not intelligent enough to listen to arguments on all sides of an issue and make up their own minds? That's demeaning to young people and is certainly a misguided view about what education should be. Education should involve the presentation of many different viewpoints to young people. Let them decide for themselves what they want to believe.

It's interesting to see what has happened since that article came out. A local newspaper, the *Newton Tab*, printed four pages of letters and an editorial about my talk, and most of the letters from students and parents were supportive.[55] I received dozens of phone calls expressing solidarity, and I have received invitations from seven different high schools asking me to speak. So, while the press focuses on the anger of people who don't want to hear antiwar speeches, there is all this antiwar sentiment that is not reported.

Some on the left are criticizing you and others, such as Noam Chomsky and Susan Sontag, for raising questions about the roots of terrorism and voicing criticisms of U.S. foreign policy.

There definitely seems to be a kind of fear that's being spread about discussing American foreign policy at this point. People object if you try to talk about what happened on September 11, and you say, "Let's examine the roots of terrorism. Let's see what's behind all of this. Let's see if there is anything in American foreign policy that has anything to do with this or if it's just caused by the fanaticism and the irrationality of the terrorists." As soon as you begin to talk about these issues, as soon as you begin to talk about American foreign policy, some editors, journalists, and politicians say, "You're justifying the terrorist attacks."

Well, that closes the arena of discussion. We only want to talk about *these* issues; we don't want to talk about those other ones. When people set an agenda and say, "We can only talk about this and we can't talk about that," they are very seriously limiting our freedom of speech. They are also creating a dangerous situation in which democracy no longer exists and there is no longer a free marketplace of opinion.

Since September 11, we have seen the creation of an atmosphere in which it becomes difficult to be critical of American foreign policy. We have to say: "I understand what happened was horrible, and terrible. We have to do all that we can to help the families of the victims. We have to do all that we can to prevent such future attacks. We must take security precautions." But let's go beyond that and see what can be done in the long-term to solve these problems.

So, I think we ought to defy the admonition to keep quiet, to stick to the agenda, to not criticize the government, to not bring up foreign policy. We have to bring up foreign policy; we have to bring up history. The one thing that enables the authorities to deceive the public is to keep the public in a state of amnesia, to keep the public from thinking back to the history of war, the history of violence, the history of government deception, the history of media complicity and deception.

If more people knew something about the history of

government deception, of the lies that were told getting us into the Mexican War, the lies that were told getting us into the Spanish-American War, the lies that were told getting us into the war in the Philippines, the lies that were told getting us into World War I, the lies that were told again and again in Vietnam, the lies on the eve of the Gulf War, they would have questions about what they are hearing from the government and the media to justify this war.

You frequently cite a saying from the journalist I. F. Stone.

I. F. Stone was one of the great journalists of our time. He would be invited to speak to students in journalism schools who were going to be reporters. He would say to them, "Among all the things I'm going to tell you today about being a journalist, all you have to remember is two words: governments lie." It's very important to know that. Otherwise we are victims of whatever the authorities say.

At a number of the teach-ins you have been speaking at, people ask you where you find the information you use in your talks. What do you tell them?

If a student asks that, I'll say: Cut class and go to the library. Cut class and go to a bookstore. Read for yourself, explore for yourself. We have to enlarge our boundaries beyond the immediate, beyond what happened on September 11, and think about how we can do away with violence in the world, how we can do away with the terrorism of fanatic sects and the terrorism of governments.

It's important not to ignore mainstream media, though. If you read the *New York Times* carefully, especially the inside pages, you will see reports that most Americans will miss and that even many readers of the *Times* will miss. Even very orthodox places like *Time*, *Newsweek*, the *Wall Street Journal*, and *Business Week* occasionally have critical reports. I remember early after September 11, I read an article in *Newsweek* magazine titled "Why Do They Hate Us?"[56] It actually laid out very specifically which American policies in the Middle East have caused so much anger against the United States.

Then we have alternative publications like *The Nation*, *In These Times*, *Z Magazine*, and *The Progressive*. *Dollars and Sense* has information about the American economy that you won't get elsewhere. The Center for Defense Information in Washington has information about the arms race, militarization, the Anti-Ballistic Missile Treaty, and nuclear proliferation that you won't get elsewhere. Amnesty International has published important information about human rights abuses, without regard to whether or not they are committed by allies or enemies of the United States. I also think it's important to read some of the smaller circulation left-wing publications that will carry information and analysis that you won't get anywhere else. The *International Socialist Review* is one of them.

I also encourage people to read Noam Chomsky's books, and other books such as Ahmed Rashid's *Taliban*, that have in-depth information about Afghanistan.[57] Or books that give an overview of American foreign policy over the last twenty or thirty years, like Stephen Shalom's book *Imperial Alibis*.[58] And the Internet is often a very good source for information that does not appear in the mainstream press.

The journalist John Reed, who wrote about the Russian Revolution in Ten Days That Shook the World ***and who organized against World War I, wrote an essay in 1917 that seems like it could have been written today, if you just replace the phrase "European melee" with the word "Afghanistan." He wrote, "War means an ugly mob madness, crucifying the truth tellers, choking the artists, sidetracking reforms, revolutions and the working of social forces. Already in America those citizens who oppose the entrance of their country into the European melee are called 'traitors,' and those who protest against the curtailing of the meager rights of free speech are spoken of as 'dangerous lunatics.'"[59]***

We have a long tradition in this country of stifling dissent exactly at those moments when dissent is badly needed. Exactly when you need free speech—when the lives of the young people in the armed forces, the lives of people overseas who may be the victims of our armed actions, are at stake—that's when they say you should shut up. Exactly when you need debate and free expression most. So you have free speech for trivial issues, and not for life-and-death issues, and that's called democracy. No, we can't accept that.

It's an old story. Tensions in foreign policy, conditions of war or near war, or "cold war," always lead to the curtailment of free speech and civil liberties in general and always create different degrees of hysteria, depending on how serious the situation is. They create an atmosphere in which it becomes possible for the government to officially limit civil liberties and also—probably even more important—to create among the citizenry an ugly mood of intolerance for dissenting voices.

While the government is limited in what it can do to control civil liberties, when the population at large internalizes the government's ideas of restriction, then any dissident is surrounded by hostile forces in the community. This goes way back to the Alien and Sedition Acts in 1798, when the United States was basically in a cold war with France. A kind of hysteria was spread about Irish revolutionaries because the Irish were rebelling, as they had been for a long time, against England. Irish immigrants had come here and were presumed to have carried dangerous revolutionary thoughts across the

Atlantic. We also had French revolutionaries in the country. Under these circumstances, Congress—with the assent of John Adams, who was recently the admired subject of a best-selling biography that passes very lightly over this—passed the Alien and Sedition Acts, which enabled the government to pick up and deport aliens without any due process or any trial, and allowed the police to jail anybody who criticized the government.[60] A small number of people were put in jail, but many more were afraid to speak out as a result.

During World War I, when John Reed made these points, there was a special need for harsh restrictions against dissent. When the United States entered World War I, there were two very powerful social groups in the country opposed to war that had the support of millions of Americans. One was the Socialist Party. Socialist newspapers were being read by maybe 2 million people in the country, and Socialists were being elected to city councils, legislatures, and even to the U.S. Congress. The second was the Industrial Workers of the World, the IWW.

The IWW and the Socialist Party were very powerful social forces in the United States that the government felt they had to suppress to successfully prepare for and carry on a war. The government undertook strenuous efforts to do this. When the United States went into war, Congress passed the Espionage Act and the Sedition Act. The Espionage Act had very little to do with espionage. Instead it made it a crime, punishable by up to twenty years in prison, to say or print anything that would "willfully obstruct the recruiting or enlistment service of the United States."[61] That was the language of the statute, which meant that if you spoke against the war, you were obviously discouraging recruitment to the armed forces of the United States and could be prosecuted.

The Sedition Act, which was an amendment to the Espionage Act, made it even a little more drastic. In fact, two thousand people were prosecuted under those acts and about a thousand went to prison. One of the people sent to jail for opposing World War I was the great socialist activist and speaker Eugene Debs. The magazine *The Masses* was put out of business, and an immense propaganda effort was undertaken to encourage Americans to look for subversives and traitors in their midst.

The First Amendment of the Constitution says that "Congress shall make no law...abridging the freedom of speech, or of the press; or the right of the people peaceably to assemble, and to petition the Government for a redress of grievances." Did this stop the Supreme Court from jailing Debs and antiwar leaders? No, they decided that maybe there are times when you can't allow freedom of speech because there is a "clear and present danger." What was the clear and present danger that the Supreme Court was facing when they made that decision? People distributing leaflets on the streets of New York opposing the draft.

Actually, Woodrow Wilson, by sending our young men

into the horror of the European war, was a clear and present danger to the nation. It's interesting. Here was the president, a presumed liberal, a Ph.D. in political science, a published historian, a former president of Princeton University, and he approved these measures. This should put to rest the notion that the more highly educated a person you have in the presidency, the wiser that person will be or the more moral that person will be. No, Wilson and Theodore Roosevelt, who was also a scholar and author, put that false notion to rest.

The distrust of foreigners generated during World War I led at the end of the war to the Palmer raids. That, too, one might say, was provoked by a terrorist act—in this case, the planting of a couple of bombs directed at Attorney General A. Mitchell Palmer. Although the government didn't know who planted the bombs, it didn't matter. This is what happens in such situations. Something happens, you don't know who did it, but you use the opportunity to act against radical people and radical organizations, which is exactly what happened in the Palmer raids. The U.S. government rounded up thousands of noncitizens, raided fraternal meeting houses and community centers where immigrants gathered, and detained these people. At one point, they marched hundreds of people manacled to one another through the streets of Boston. Then they put people on ships and deported them. Among the two most famous deportees were the anarchists Emma Goldman and Alexander Berkman.

I think it's fair to say that the very important death-penalty case of the Italian anarchists Nicola Sacco and Bartolomeo Vanzetti, which began in 1921, a few years after the war, was also connected to the wartime hysteria. The patriotism of World War I was still a factor. In fact, the newspapers at the time were full of reports about the bodies of dead soldiers returning from Europe. And the jurors in the Sacco and Vanzetti case were allowed to read the newspapers. The fact that Sacco and Vanzetti were anarchists and also foreigners, I think, had a lot do with their conviction and execution.

In his address on the meaning of the Fourth of July to blacks, the abolitionist leader Frederick Douglass made some very interesting comments about dissent. "To say now that America was right, and England wrong, is exceedingly easy. Everybody can say it; the dastard, not less than the noble brave, can flippantly discant on the tyranny of England towards the American Colonies. It is fashionable to do so; but there was a time when, to pronounce against England, and in favor of the cause of the colonies, tried men's souls. They who did so were accounted in their day plotters of mischief, agitators and rebels, dangerous men. To side with the right against the wrong, with the weak against the strong, and with the oppressed against the oppressor! [H]ere lies the merit, and the one which, of all others, seems unfashionable in our day. The cause of liberty may [today] be stabbed by the men who glory in the deeds of your [fore]fathers."[62]

Douglass is talking about how fashionable it is to go along with authority, and how dissenters in one situation may suppress dissent in another. The American revolutionaries who rebelled against England soon became guardians of the status quo, that is, protectors of slavery and a ruling elite themselves.

In the United States we have come a long way from our revolutionary history, from the time when the colonists engaged in civil disobedience against England, and the Declaration of Independence set forth the principle that governments are artificial entities, which, if they do not protect the equal right to life, liberty, and the pursuit of happiness, must be "altered or abolished."

Just a few years after the victorious war for independence, the new American government became a counter-revolutionary force. Indeed, the Constitution itself was framed in an atmosphere of fear of rebellion, with the Shays Rebellion in western Massachusetts sounding an alarm bell for the Founding Fathers.

As for other countries wanting independence, just as the American colonies did, it became clear that there would be no tolerance of other wars for independence now that we had won ours. Thus, the black rebels of Haiti, fighting successfully against French rule, and winning, were opposed by the administration of Thomas

Jefferson, ironically the man who had written the Declaration of Independence. The United States refused to recognize the new republic of Haiti for more than half a century.

In the decades before the Civil War, and this was in Frederick Douglass's time, persons expressing abolitionist opinions were in danger of their lives, and when black and white opponents of slavery helped fugitive slaves, they were prosecuted.

The warning of Frederick Douglass, that the political leaders who mouth platitudes of admiration for the Founding Fathers will "stab" the liberties of the American people, is being borne out today, during the war on Afghanistan. Recognizing that should spur those of us who believe in freedom to resist the destruction of our liberties.

President Bush signed an executive order on November 13, 2001, that authorizes new military tribunals for suspected terrorists. He said he was fighting "against the most evil kinds of people, and I need to have that extraordinary option at my fingertips." Under the order, the secret tribunals can "find a defendant guilty even if a third of the officers disagree, and execute the alien with no review by any civilian court."[63]

We've always had military courts for the trial of military people, but the idea of military courts for civilians is new and is really a very, very dangerous idea. It's a way of simply taking away people's constitutional rights. Even noncitizens are supposed to have constitutional rights. But these rights disappear as soon as you put people before a military tribunal.

The Bush executive order introduces the use of secret trials. That's what happens in military dictatorships that we profess to be aghast at. But here we are preparing for secret trials with secret evidence and no unanimity required on the part of juries. This is really a situation that Americans should be protesting loudly. But here, too, in the atmosphere created by what happened on September 11, and played up by the Bush administration and the mass media in the most shameful way, the administration can say it's going to try people in military courts, and the number of voices raised against this so far is very small.

Only a handful of voices in the press rose against this. I noticed in the paper this morning that Kerry Kennedy Cuomo went to this commemoration of her father, Robert Kennedy, which George Bush was attending. Bush and the others were paying homage to Robert Kennedy and were naming the Justice Department headquarters after him. You know, hypocrisy never sleeps in Washington. And she spoke to reporters, criticizing this new assault on civil liberties. It was very, very bold of her. But not very many voices have been raised.[64]

William Safire, with whom we rarely have occasion to agree, also wrote a column calling the military tribunals "Orwellian." He said Bush's "kangaroo court can conceal evidence by citing national security, [and] make up its own rules.... [N]on-citizens face an executive that is now investigator, prosecutor, judge, jury and jailer or executioner. In an Orwellian twist, Bush's order calls this Soviet-style abomination 'a full and fair trial.'"[65]

That was remarkable. I guess Safire's proper role as a journalist came alive for that brief moment.

President Bush signed another executive order after September 11 that I expect would be of special concern to you as a historian. He has made it far harder for people to gain access to presidential papers. According to the New York Times, *the November 1 order "allow[s] a sitting president to keep secret the papers of a previous president, even if a previous president wants his papers made public."[66]*

The Freedom of Information Act was one of the remarkable gains that came out of the 1960s. It has been tremendously useful for scholars and for citizens who want to find out more about what our government and what our presidents have done. It's very instructive for American people to learn what motivated our presidents in making their decisions, and that's why Bush is obviously trying to clamp down on public access to government records.

So much of this reminds me of Stalinism, really. You wipe out history; you close the books. Stalin did not want the Russian people to know who was involved in the Russian Revolution because he was killing off the leaders of the Russian Revolution. In this case, I think Bush does not want the American people to learn the crass motives behind the decisions of American presidents.

Maybe he was led to this by the public disclosure of facts that we recently learned through the opening up of the tapes of John F. Kennedy, Lyndon Johnson, and Richard Nixon. We've learned how little we can trust the government to act upon decent motives. We learned that Kennedy was willing to make a decision about whether or not to pull troops out of Vietnam based on his election chances in 1964. Johnson was also making crucial decisions about whether the United States would escalate the war in Vietnam based on his own political future.

Johnson told Richard Russell, a Senator from Georgia, a very conservative man who turned out in the case of the Vietnam War to be cautioning Johnson, that he knew a lot of people would be killed in Vietnam. But, he said, "[T]hey would impeach a president that would run out, wouldn't they?"[67] Talk about courage. Johnson would rather go into a war, would rather sacrifice the lives of countless people, than face the possibility that he might be removed from office.

And then we have seen in these tapes numerous revelations about Nixon and his rabid anti-Semitism, among other issues.

Bush does not want the American people to know how their government works. Kids go to junior high school and they get textbooks with diagrams illustrating the structure of the U.S. government, with its "checks and balances." But that's not the real story, and if Bush has his way, we're not going to learn how governments really function.

The **New York Times** *also recently reported some new revelations about Johnson's knowledge that the Gulf of Tonkin incident was fabricated.*[68] *Is this really new information or is it just being acknowledged by the* **Times** *after the fact?*

Well, it was news that Johnson himself had doubts about the Gulf of Tonkin. What was not news was that the supposed attack on the destroyer *Maddox* was fabricated, that the attack on the destroyer *Turner Jay* was dubious, and that these destroyers were part of a spy operation against North Vietnam, not at all on a "routine mission," as was officially claimed. That has not been news for a long time.

After the so-called incident in the Gulf of Tonkin in August 1964, people from the U.S. government got up before the microphones and lied again and again to the

Howard Zinn

American people about what had happened. Johnson, Robert McNamara, Dean Rusk. All of them lied. Their statements led to Congress passing the Tonkin resolution, which gave Johnson carte blanche to do what he wanted in Southeast Asia.

It's one thing to say that we learned that the incident was all a fake; it is another thing to learn that the president knew it was a fake, or at least suspected it was a fake.

WAR ON CIVILIANS

In his book Century of War, *Gabriel Kolko writes, "Warfare after 1937 has increasingly eliminated the distinction between combatants and others...traumatizing more and more civilians and entire nations." According to an article in the* Boston Review, *"up to 35 million people—90 percent civilians—have been killed in 170 wars since the end of World War II."*[69]

Kolko is certainly right that war has increasingly become war against civilians. In World War I, the ratio of military personnel to civilians dying was probably ten to one. After World War I, war becomes a matter of the bombardment of cities. This becomes very clear in World War II. Though many people died on the battlefield, probably more people died in concentration camps, in prison camps, and in the massive bombing of Dresden, Frankfurt, and Hamburg. One hundred thousand died alone one night in the firebombing of Tokyo. Add in the more than two hundred thousand civilians who were killed in Hiroshima and Nagasaki, Japan, and the ratio begins to turn the other way, toward more and more civilian deaths.

During the Vietnam War, far more civilians died than

military personnel. The same was true in the Korean War. Most Americans have no idea what we did in Korea, but Korea was really a preview of Vietnam, particularly in the use of napalm and the bombing of villages, which contributed to more than 2 million people dying, most of them civilians.

War is now largely a war against people who are not combatants. And for that reason alone, war cannot be accepted in any judgment of what is to be done to resolve problems in international relations.

In Catholic theology and in philosophical theory about war, which is sometimes called "just war theory," people used to cite something called "the principle of proportionality." The Geneva Convention also includes language on this point (see Appendix A). This was a very important principle in deciding whether a war was just or unjust. But when war becomes a war against civilians, and when war uses the enormous destructive technology now available, it inevitably becomes something of frightening proportions. This is true even when we are talking about small wars—and we've had a number of so-called small wars since World War II, wars that only killed 1 million people, like the Iran-Iraq war or the civil war in Nigeria.

So, war itself becomes unacceptable and unjust because the principle of proportionality is immediately violated by the fact that the technology is so massive and the killing of innocent people is inevitable.

You mentioned to me a while ago that you're reading a book by the Swedish writer Sven Lindqvist called A History of Bombing. *He writes that during World War I, "the military looked desperately for a new, more mobile way to wage war. Aerial combat seemed to offer the most obvious solution; attacks against the civilian population would force rapid results and ultimate victories."*[70]

It's an interesting book. Lindqvist goes back to World War I, when bombing actually started on a pretty important scale, although of course nothing like what happened later. One of the most important things he does is to remind us—or to inform those people who don't know, and I suppose a lot of people don't know this—how deliberate was the decision to bomb civilian populations in World War II. Arthur Harris, who was head of the Bomber Command in England, Winston Churchill, and Churchill's advisers made the conscious decision to terrorize the working-class populations of German cities, thinking that they would destroy the morale of the German people and win the war.[71]

In World War II, in general the British bombed at night and the Americans bombed in the daytime. The bombing at night was very specifically carpet bombing because the RAF had no way of knowing what they were bombing. They had no compunction after this decision was made about carpet bombing Dresden, Hamburg, Frankfurt, and the other cities.

Howard Zinn

The Americans pretended to be more precise. We had the Norden bombsight and were bombing in the daytime.[72] Presumably we were being more accurate and only bombing military targets. But I can tell you from my own experience as a bombardier during World War II, the Norden bombsight was not accurate at four thousand feet and even less accurate at eleven thousand feet. But we bombed from thirty thousand feet, and when a bomb is dropped from that height, there is no way you can identify and hit only military targets. Your bombs will go all over the place, within a quarter of a mile. So, it was a pretense that we were doing precision bombing. We were killing civilians.

In *A History of Bombing*, Lindqvist points out that Curtis LeMay, who later became the head of the U.S. Strategic Air Command, went to Europe and saw what Arthur Harris was doing. "Hamburg and Dresden showed [LeMay] what could be accomplished."[73] So, LeMay observed this tactic of bombing civilian populations and then went to the Pacific, where he was in charge of the decision to bomb Tokyo. The bombing set Tokyo aflame in that one terrible night in the spring of 1945, and a hundred thousand people died. And years later in the Vietnam War, it was Curtis LeMay, having learned his lesson from Arthur Harris, who said about Vietnam, "[W]e're going to bomb them back into the Stone Ages."[74]

But the claim is made that we now have "smart bombs," guided missiles that precisely hit their targets.

The claim that smart bombs and technology now enable pinpoint bombing is very much a fraud. They discovered after the Gulf War that 93 percent of the bombs turned out not to be so-called smart bombs and that the "smart" bombs often missed their targets. Overall, 70 percent of our bombs missed their targets.[75]

The United States dropped 88,500 tons of bombs on Iraq during the forty-three days of the war, with the goal of, as the *Washington Post* put it, "disabling Iraqi society at large." According to the reporter Barton Gellman:

> Some targets, especially late in the war, were bombed primarily to create postwar leverage over Iraq.... Military planners hoped the bombing would amplify the economic and psychological impact of international sanctions on Iraqi society.... Because of these goals, damage to civilian structures and interests, invariably described by briefers during the war as "collateral" and unintended, was sometimes neither.[76]

So, the result was wreaking havoc on Iraq and killing civilians with so-called smart bombs. We see this very clearly now in Afghanistan. Our planes are bombing from high altitudes because they want to escape anti-aircraft fire. When you bomb at high altitudes, with whatever sophisticated equipment, you are not really in a position to be sure what you're hitting. You don't see anything on the ground. You see flashes and explosions, but you don't hear screams, you don't see blood, you don't see severed limbs. You don't see any of that.

In Afghanistan, villages are being bombed; residential areas are being bombed. In today's paper—and it's always buried on the inside pages—Afghan people describe how their mud homes had been destroyed by American bombs. The United States bombed a Red Cross building in Afghanistan not once, but twice, even though its roof is clearly marked with the Red Cross symbol and its location was well known. President Bush wants us to donate to the Red Cross, but he should at least assure us that the U.S. military won't bomb the Red Cross. A third missile was targeted at the same Red Cross site, even after the United States had apologized for the first attack, but, according to the *New York Times*, "One of the American aircraft that had been ordered to hit the Red Cross supply warehouses missed its target and hit a residential neighborhood instead."[77]

The United States also hit and killed four Afghans who were risking their lives working in cooperation with the United Nations to remove mines. A cousin of one of the men who was killed told the *Boston Globe*, "They are not God. They want to pinpoint every target, but they can't make every missile go after Osama [bin Laden] and terrorist training camps."[78]

So, it's clear that all the talk about smart bombs is an

attempt—and I'm afraid, a largely successful attempt—to convince the American public that we are humane in our bombing. This is very important. The concealment of what we're doing to the population in Afghanistan is essential. Most people—and not because they have any theories about just war—make a kind of common sense calculation, a moral calculation. And if they knew that we were killing large numbers of people, and displacing hundreds of thousands of people from their homes, they would not take such a benign view of the Afghan war. They would not simply go along with their government. So, it becomes very important for the government to conceal the human effects of our bombing. And if you conceal that from the American population, then it's possible to understand why people would think we are not doing much harm, and therefore it is worth attacking Afghanistan if it leads to the elimination of terrorism.

What have those human effects been?

It's clear that civilians are being killed in the bombing. I read an account of one attack on the town of Gudara on December 1. "The village is no more," a survivor of the attack said. "All my family, twelve people, were killed. I am the only one left in this family. I have lost my children, my wife. They are no more."[79]

But these reports are mostly out of sight of the general public and are virtually never reported on national television, where most Americans get their news, and they're so dispersed that they reinforce the idea that the bombing of civilians is an infrequent event, an accident, an unfortunate mistake. Walter Isaacson, the chief executive of CNN, told his staff that it was "perverse to focus too much on the casualties or hardship in Afghanistan." And an executive at the Panama City *News Herald* told the staff, "*Do not use* photos on Page 1 showing civilian casualties from the U.S. war in Afghanistan" because a sister paper had received complaints.[80]

The Pentagon has been deliberately downplaying the truth about casualties. In response to a report from the United Nations that U.S. planes had bombed a mosque near Herat, Victoria Clarke, a Pentagon spokeswoman, said, "We take extraordinary care on the targeting process. Our targets are military. Our targets are al-Qaeda. That's what we are going after. There is unintended damage. There is collateral damage. Thus far, it has been extremely limited from what we have seen."[81]

Pentagon officials confidently assert these denials half a world away in Washington. The *Washington Post* described how "[a]lmost all the information [about the war in Afghanistan] has been released from the Pentagon, far away from the conflict, and much of it has been dated and vague." I am reminded of what General Colin Powell, Bush's secretary of state who was then the chairman of the Joint Chiefs of Staff, said when he was asked about the number of Iraqis killed during the

Gulf War. He said, "It's really not a number I'm terribly interested in."[82]

But on-the-spot press reports from the villages, from hospitals where the wounded lie, and from the Pakistan border where refugees have fled the bombs reveal a different story. According to a report from Agence France-Presse,

> Refugees arriving in Pakistan...recounted how twenty people, including nine children, had been killed as they tried to flee an attack on the southern Afghan town of Tirin Kot on a tractor and trailer.
>
> One survivor, Abdul Maroof, 28, said injured people were left screaming in vain for help after the tractor was bombed on a remote rural road, far from the nearest hospital.
>
> Refugees from Herat, who traveled for six days to get to the eastern border with Pakistan, told of horrifying destruction along the main road to Kandahar.
>
> "Kandahar was completely destroyed. Everything has turned into a pile of stones...," said refugee Abdul Nabi.[83]

I read a chilling account in the *Boston Globe* about the intensive care unit at Jalalabad Public Hospital, filled with "the victims of American bombing" who "bore the look of disbelief on their blood-speckled faces":

> In one bed lay Noor Mohammad, 10, who was a bundle of bandages. He lost his eyes and hands to the bomb that hit his house after Sunday dinner. Hospital director Guloja Shimwari shook his head at the boy's wounds.

"The United States must be thinking he is Osama," Shimwari said. "If he is not Osama, then why would they do this?"

... The hospital's morgue received 17 bodies last weekend, and officials here estimate at least 89 civilians were killed in several villages.

In the hospital yesterday, a bomb's damage could be chronicled in the life of one family. A bomb had killed the father, Faisal Karim. In one bed was his wife, Mustafa Jama, who had severe head injuries.

... Around her, six of her children were in bandages. They ranged from 18-year-old Brishna to 10-month-old Raheem. One of them, Zahidullah, 8, lay in a coma.[84]

Barry Bearak, reporting on December 15, 2001, from the village of Madoo, Afghanistan, described the destruction of fifteen houses, "obliterated into splintered wood and dust by American bombs," killing fifty-five people. "In the night, as we slept, they dropped the bombs on us," said Paira Gul, who lost his sisters and their families in the attack. "Most of the dead are children," another villager said. But as Bearak notes, "most likely, [the people of] Madoo will not learn whether the bombs fell by mistake or on purpose, and the matter will be forgotten amid the larger consequences of the war."[85]

I am quoting from a few of the reports that journalists were able to get out under tremendously difficult conditions. The *Washington Post* said that "reporters have operated under limitations even more restrictive than those imposed on [journalist] pools during the Persian Gulf War in 1991." On December 5, journalists were at Camp Rhino, a Marine base in Afghanistan, when the news came in that U.S. soldiers had been killed in a "friendly fire" incident. A B-52 bomber had killed two U.S. fighters. Even though the bodies were brought back to the compound, just a hundred yards from where the journalists were being housed, they were denied access to the wounded and weren't allowed to take photographs.[86]

So, when we read the reports in the foreign press or on the wires, or the occasional story in the mainstream press, about innocent people who are being bombed, we have to think about all the incidents that aren't being reported. We have to think of all the stories that we haven't been told.

We also have to ask another question: "Is it really an accident when civilians die under our bombs?" Even if you believe the Pentagon's claim that its intention is not to kill civilians, if civilians in fact become victims again and again, and it's predictable that they will, can that be called an accident? If the deaths of civilians are inevitable in bombing, as Donald Rumsfeld acknowledged, it is not an accident. The people prosecuting this war are committing murder. They are engaging in terrorism.[87]

In 1998, you had an interesting correspondence with an Iraqi doctor who was living in London, Mohammed Al-Obaidi.

Howard Zinn

Yes, in December 1998, I received an e-mail from London. That month there was a particular intensity to the U.S. bombing of Iraq, and this e-mail came to me out of the blue from Dr. Al-Obaidi. I think he had read something that I had written, and he told me that he had left Iraq because Saddam Hussein had killed his father and his brother. He left Iraq and moved to London to take up his medical practice. He said he was writing to me because just a few days before, an American cruise missile had struck the home of his mother, who was living on the outskirts of Baghdad, and killed her and his sister-in-law, the widow of his brother who had been killed by Saddam Hussein, and their three kids. As he put it, Saddam Hussein and Bill Clinton had, together, wiped out his family.[88]

I sent that story out on the Internet to disseminate it as widely as I could because I thought it might have the same effect on other people it had on me. The abstract notion of the United States bombing Iraq really had very little meaning for me until I read a human story of one person and one family. This is a fundamental problem that we have in reading the news and reading about bombing. When you see statistics about how many people died, the reality does not really strike us, until we see it presented in one or two human beings.

One reason that all of us were so shocked and upset and terrified by what happened in New York and Washington on September 11 is that we saw these victims up close, again and again. We saw the piles of rubble and people leaping out of windows. And we saw the faces of the people who were racing from the disaster. One of the things that occurred to me, after I had gotten over my initial reaction of shock and horror at what had been done, was that other scenes of horror have taken place in other parts of the world and they just never meant very much to us.

I thought also about the fact that when I was a bombardier in the air force, dropping bombs from thirty thousand feet, I did not see any human beings. It occurred to me that scenes like the ones that appeared on televisions, the scenes from New York and Washington, must have been taking place down below in these cities in Europe that I was bombing, but it didn't mean anything to me. I was engaged in a "good war." I was doing something. I was on the right side. There is always a right side and a wrong side in war, and it is your side that is the right side. And once you have decided that you are on the right side, then anything goes. It does not matter what happens to anybody else.

Just like, no doubt, the people who carried out the unconscionable attacks of September 11 felt.

Yes, they have some cause, they feel they are on the right side, and therefore the people who died—those three thousand people who were crushed and burned and died—are just ciphers for them. Just as the hundreds of thousands of victims in Iraq are ciphers to us; just as the people in Hiroshima and Nagasaki were ciphers to Harry Truman. We should also remember that Truman called Hiroshima a military target. When Truman announced the bombing, he said, "The world will note that the first atomic bomb was dropped on Hiroshima, a military base. That was because we wished in this first attack to avoid, insofar as possible, the killing of civilians." I remembered this when I read a quote from Lieutenant Colonel Dave Lapan at the Pentagon, who was asked about civilians killed in Afghanistan. He said, "Were civilians killed? Possibly. If they were killed, it was because they were in the vicinity of a military target."[89]

6

THE LOGIC OF WAR

Rolling Stone *magazine asked you what you would put in a time capsule for the future. You had a very interesting answer. You said Bob Dylan's song "Masters of War."*[90]

I just recently listened to "Masters of War," in fact driving in the car this morning. "Masters of War" would be a good addition to a time capsule. I would also want to put in some of Dylan's other songs, which say so much. His songs about George Jackson, Hurricane Carter, and Emmett Till are haunting, powerful songs. They tell about our time and our civilization in a shocking way.[91]

I saw Dylan perform the other night in Boston and he played two other antiwar songs: "Blowin' in the Wind," with the haunting line "Yes, 'n' how many deaths will it take till he knows / That too many people have died?" and "John Brown." "John Brown" tells the story of a soldier who comes back disfigured from fighting in a war and meets his mother at the train station:

> Don't you remember, Ma, when I went off to war
> You thought it was the best thing I could do?

I was on the battleground, you were home…acting proud.
You wasn't there standing in my shoes.

Oh, and I thought when I was there, God, what am I doing
  here?
I'm a-tryin' to kill somebody or die tryin'.
But the thing that scared me most was when my enemy
  came close
And I saw that his face looked just like mine.[92]

I guess we also have to include in that time capsule other more positive and more uplifting stories, as well. Maybe some of the songs of Pete Seeger, Bruce Springsteen, and Ani DiFranco, songs that celebrate what people do in resisting oppression.

Another Bob Dylan song seems especially timely right now: "With God on Our Side." George Bush recently said "God is not neutral in this conflict." The Bush administration seems to think it has God on its side, just like Osama bin Laden has God on his side.[93]

Well, if God were not neutral, then Bush would be gone…but I've never checked up really on God's neutrality.

The invoking of God has actually been done by all American presidents. Given the so-called separation of church and state, it's really ironic that every president seems absolutely obsessed with calling upon God to bless us. Ronald Reagan wrote, "Perhaps no custom reveals our character as a nation so clearly as our celebration of Thanksgiving Day. Rooted deeply in our Judeo-Christian heritage, the practice of offering thanksgiving underscores our unshakable belief in God as the foundation of our nation and our firm reliance upon Him from Whom all blessings flow."[94] But Bush is invoking God more than anybody else. And then when you join this to his talk about a "crusade" against whoever perpetrated the attack on September 11, then it puts the United States in a position of a crusading country with God on our side.[95]

It's interesting that God is brought into the picture when the government is doing great violence. Maybe it's when you are doing great violence that you desperately need some support. You're not going to get any moral support from any thinking person, but since God isn't thinking at the moment, maybe you can pull out God to support you. He certainly isn't around to contradict you.

It's a pernicious thing to do. It takes advantage of the fact that a lot of people in this country believe in God, go to church, and think of God as a moral force. Then you use God to support the most immoral of acts, which is war.

Eugene Debs wrote in a letter to the New York Sun *in 1915, "If...the United States were to prove in good faith that it is opposed to the barbarism and butchery of war by issuing a proclamation of peace, and itself setting the example of disarmament to the nations of the world, its preparedness would be, not only in accordance with its vaunted ideals, but a thousandfold greater guarantee to the respect of its neighbors and to its own security and peace than if it were loaded down with all the implements of death and destruction on earth."*[96]

Debs was talking about "preparedness" because the war in Europe had begun and, although the United States was not yet in the war, people were beginning to talk about preparedness for war. The American military is building up, and Debs sees this coming. He argues that the best thing we can do is to declare our belief in peace and to stop preparedness for war. You prepare for war, and then the momentum is created for going to war. We have seen that repeatedly.

Debs is also questioning the idea that spending more money on arms, or on "defense," is a way to preserve peace. This has echoes in the renewed debate about a national missile defense shield.

Yes, the Bush administration is calling for missile defense. Not only the administration but the Democratic Party, which is only theoretically a party of opposition but actually, and especially in matters of foreign policy, always goes along with whatever the government policy is. The Democrats are going along with the idea of a missile shield even though they have in the past criticized the Star Wars program and pointed out what scientists have been saying again and again: that it simply does not work. The tests that have been designed to prove that missile defense works have only proved that it doesn't work.

Then you have another very compelling argument against the missile defense: By scrapping the 1972 Anti-Ballistic Missile Treaty with Russia, you are creating the possibility of a greater arms race. You are challenging other nations to develop weaponry that can bypass the national missile defense shield. The history of arms technology is that whenever you have a development in defensive technology, you soon have another development in offensive technology to overcome that. The French built the Maginot line, which was supposed to protect them against the German invasion, and by the time they had built the Maginot line, it was out of date.

Missile defense is fundamentally a program to make profits for the corporations that are going to get the billions of dollars in contracts to build the system. This is an enormous theft from the American people. Remember the quote from Eisenhower. He said, "Every gun that is made, every warship launched, every rocket fired, signifies, in the final sense, a theft from those who hunger and are not fed, those who are cold and are not clothed. The world in arms is not spending money alone. It is spending the sweat of its laborers, the genius of its scientists, the hopes of its children."[97]

Rosa Luxemburg, the Polish revolutionary, wrote in 1911 that "militarism in both its forms—as war and as armed peace—is a legitimate child, a logical result of capitalism."[98] *Is there a connection between war and the way the economy is managed under capitalism?*

Certainly there is a connection between capitalism and war. That doesn't mean that it is an exclusive connection. We have had wars before capitalism, and we've had wars engaged in by governments that are precapitalist. We've had wars engaged in by the Soviet Union, which was not really a socialist state, and not quite the traditional capitalist state; sometimes it has been described as "state capitalism."

While you don't have to have a capitalist society to have war, certainly capitalism feeds upon war, and war feeds upon capitalism. As soon as you have societies driven by profit, you are in a situation of nations vying for exploitation of other peoples and other materials. Then nations competing for that profit are going to engage in war with one another. You see how many wars are fought over colonies, raw materials, and cheap labor. That's what imperialism is.

So, by being based on profit, capitalism certainly makes wars between nations, wars over economic resources, much more likely, indeed, inevitable.

Then you have another fact about capitalism: Under capitalism, corporations that produce weapons make huge profits from these weapons of war and therefore are happy both to prepare for war and to engage in war. You prepare for war, you have all these government contracts, and make all this money, and then you engage in war and you use up all these products and you have to replace them.

So yes, the connection between capitalism and war is a close one, and I suspect that if we can build a world without capitalism, without the principle of profit being dominant, we may not eliminate all conflict or violence or war, but we would have gone a long way toward that goal.

Howard Zinn

7

NOT IN OUR NAME

The United States has a long history of antiwar activism and pacifism.

It's a long history. It's not always a victorious history, in that antiwar movements have only very rarely succeeded in having an effect on the makers of war, but we certainly have had internal movements against war from the American Revolution to today. There were mutinies in the American army against the officers by soldiers disillusioned with the war and the class nature of the war—with their own misery and the luxurious treatment of the officers.

When the Mexican War takes place from 1846 to 1848, you also see desertions from the U.S. Army. Many of the people who were in the army in the Mexican War were recent immigrants. There was a whole regiment of Irish immigrants in the Mexican War. As soon as many of these soldiers enter the war, they see the mayhem and become disillusioned. In fact, a number of them desert to the Mexicans and form the San Patricio Battalion, St. Patrick's Battalion. Every year, Mexicans celebrate the heroes of the San Patricio Battalion.

The Civil War was much more complex because it was both a war against slavery and a war to establish the dominance of the Northern industrial and financial interests by unifying the country into one profitable market. So, a war with this moral element, the elimination of slavery, at the same time is not a war that all working-class people can support, because they resent its class character. The rich can get out of the war by paying three hundred dollars. That becomes the root of the draft riots that take place in New York and several other cities in 1863, which are some of the greatest internal uprisings in American history.

Then you have the Spanish-American war.

Yes, the public is whipped up into a frenzy against Spain. The lie is told that the U.S.S. *Maine,* which was docked in Havana harbor, was blown up by the Spanish. No one asked what the *Maine* was doing in Cuba, but this becomes a cause for war. (By the way, years later, it was revealed that the *Maine* exploded because of a defect in its engine.) So, the war lasts a very short time, and there wasn't much time for an antiwar movement to develop.

But the Spanish-American War is quickly followed by the war in the Philippines, which lasts for years, and an antiwar movement develops. Mark Twain and some other very distinguished Americans form the Anti-Imperialist League. Some of the black soldiers sent to the

Philippines desert and go over to the other side to fight with the Filipinos, with whom they feel they have a greater rapport than they had with their white officers.

Twain wrote scathing essays about the war in the Philippines and U.S. imperialism.

Yes, Twain wrote some wonderful pieces. One essay he wrote was called "The War Prayer":

> O Lord our God, help us to tear their soldiers to bloody shreds with our shells; help us to cover their smiling fields with the pale forms of their patriot dead; help us to drown the thunder of the guns with the shrieks of their wounded, writhing in pain; help us to lay waste their humble homes with a hurricane of fire; help us to wring the hearts of their unoffending widows with unavailing grief; help us to turn them out roofless with their little children to wander unfriended the wastes of their desolated land in rags and hunger and thirst.[99]

By World War I, the antiwar movement had grown much larger.

Yes, in World War I, there was a very substantial movement against the war, despite the government's repression. Even during World War II, we saw people speak out against the war. As with the Civil War, World War II had a moral element that was hard to extricate from the crass motives of the people who organized the war effort. Yes, we wanted to fight Hitler and fascism. We were witnessing the murder of the Jews and others, and the aggression against other countries. But all of that is mixed in with something much less noble, and that is the desire of the Western powers—who themselves had been expansionist and brutal, and had been creating colonies all over the world—to keep the Japanese and Germans out of the areas of the world that they wanted to control. Some people in the United States, admittedly a small minority, understood this and opposed the war. There was right-wing and isolationist opposition to World War II, some of it even pro-Nazi, but another part of it was pacifist. About six thousand Americans went to jail for refusing to fight in World War II.

World War II still remains the "good war" in the American mind. Yet there are troubling memories: the bombing of Hiroshima and Nagasaki, the revelation that we had caused perhaps a hundred thousand casualties in the bombing of Dresden, and the fact that we'd engaged in the ruthless bombing of civilians. It was the "good war," but it ended without the elimination of racism, or tyranny, or aggression in the world. Hitler and Japan and Mussolini were defeated, but now we had two superpowers—both of which were eventually armed with nuclear weapons—fighting for control of various parts of the world.

I said that it was rare for an antiwar movement to have any real effect on American policy, but Vietnam was the outstanding exception. In Vietnam, the war lasted long enough for the American people to see behind the deceptions of the government and begin to learn about the atrocities being committed against the Vietnamese people.

Many GIs turned against the war and formed organizations such as Vietnam Veterans Against the War. So, while in 1966 about two-thirds of the American people supported the war, by 1969 about two-thirds opposed the war. That's a very dramatic turnaround. For the first time, there was an antiwar movement powerful enough to have an impact on government policy.

You can see this effect by reading the internal memos of the government. If you read the Pentagon Papers—which were not supposed to be seen by the American people, but which were released as an act of civil disobedience in 1971—you see how fearful the administration was about antiwar protests. The government understood how difficult it would be to carry on the war with all the defections, the refusals to be drafted, the closing down of ROTC chapters, and the general opposition to the war. They were also worried about the black uprisings in the cities in 1967 and 1968, which were not specifically directed against the war but were connected. The escalation of the war in Vietnam meant the neglect of the condition of the people in the black ghettoes in the United States, a connection that was explicitly made by Martin Luther King Jr.

So, with the Vietnam War we saw the first antiwar movement that became broad enough and strong enough to have an effect on governmental policy. And apparently the government learned something from that war. It learned that if it's going to conduct a war, it must finish it quickly, before an antiwar movement develops.

You've written that opposition to the Vietnam War started out among a small minority and then, through hard and patient work, became a national and effective movement. How does the antiwar movement today look in light of this historical example?

Clearly things have started faster here in actions against the war. Even before we were at war, before the bombing had started, people had organized teach-ins, rallies, demonstrations, and so on. In the case of Vietnam, it took longer for things to develop. I remember the spring of 1965, when the first big bombing of Vietnam began, we held an antiwar rally, the first antiwar rally on the Boston Common, and a hundred people showed up. This past September, even before the bombing of Afghanistan had begun, we had a rally in Copley Square in Boston and a thousand people showed up. Thousands more in San Francisco and in New York City demonstrated against war. So, the momentum certainly started faster in this war than it did during Vietnam.

A number of people have speculated that the Bush administration is trying to kick the "Vietnam syn-

drome" in this war, to give greater legitimacy to U.S. militarism.

The Vietnam syndrome is an interesting phenomenon. Presumably the Vietnam syndrome refers to the fact that we fought a long war in Vietnam, which turned into a more and more unpopular war that the American people finally did not support. As a result, the American government had to withdraw ignominiously but obviously with the determination not to allow this defeat to be repeated again or to stand as a sign of the weakness of the American empire. So, the notion of a Vietnam syndrome became bandied about, this fear of engaging in a war that the American people would not support.

I think the ghost of Vietnam still remains. Americans are generally reluctant to go to war until the president goes into action and then the media go into action and they create an atmosphere in which war seems justified. The *New York Times* had an article asking if the United States was getting into "another Vietnam" in Afghanistan. And the *Times* ran a very interesting letter from a former officer at the American Embassy in Vietnam about the announcement that the U.S. government was sending more "advisers" into Afghanistan. He asked, "Are we now in for the same kind of subterfuge until we have another six-figure number of combat troops searching the caves of Afghanistan—with perhaps an equally distressing consequence?" And now the

United States is sending "advisers," including eighty-five
U.S. Special Forces training officers who have been "dis-
patched to help battle an Islamic insurgency," to the
Philippines. The *Boston Globe* wrote that "[t]o
Americans who remember the origins of the U.S. war in
Vietnam, there is something unnerving about the news
that the Pentagon is sending 660 military advisers to help
Philippine armed forces overcome the radical Islamic
group known as Abu Sayyaf."[100]

So, immediately after the Vietnam War, the U.S. government methodically set about trying to eliminate the
Vietnam syndrome, that is, trying to make wars palatable
once again, as they had been after World War II. For many
people, war was no longer acceptable, and the government had to do something to make war acceptable again.

In fact, the very year that the war in Vietnam ended,
the United States undertook military actions that were
intended to bolster pride in its power. One of the first
opportunities was the *Mayaguez* affair, a small, now-for-
gotten incident in American history. Toward the end of
the Vietnam War, in May 1975, Cambodia detained an
American merchant vessel, the *Mayaguez*, with its crew.
Here was tiny Cambodia detaining an American merchant ship. The Cambodian government said the ship
was in their waters and that they had a right to detain it.
Immediately the United States went into action, even
though it had no evidence that the Cambodians were
mistreating the crew.

Gerald Ford was the president. Henry Kissinger, his adviser, had been saying for some time that the United States needed to do something to restore its prestige in the world. Kissinger always associated prestige with military prowess. And so the United States immediately set out on a military campaign, presumably to free the sailors of the *Mayaguez*. They went into a frenzy and bombarded a little island, Tang Island, where it was mistakenly thought the sailors were kept. One might ask: "Why do you want to bombard an island if you think the sailors are being kept there?"

Then U.S. marines invaded the island. In the meantime, the *Mayaguez* sailors were on their way back to freedom. The Cambodian government had already released the sailors, but the Americans were invading Tang Island and more than forty Americans died in the invasion.[101] That absolutely stupid kind of military intervention was all designed to show that the United States is still strong, as if being able to bully tiny Cambodia is a sign of being a great power.

And then we have more attempts to undo the so-called Vietnam syndrome, like when President Reagan invades Grenada in the first years of his administration. Again, it's sort of laughable. You pick on some very tiny place that you can very clearly dominate in order to show that you are tough. So, we invade Grenada using all sorts of subterfuges, and excuses, which turn out to be false.

The Gulf War was a more serious attempt to undo the Vietnam syndrome. Unlike the *Mayaguez* affair or the invasion of Grenada, the Gulf War was a full-scale military assault. The government took great pains to make sure that it did not have the same result as the war in Vietnam, that is, the building up of an antiwar movement. Although Iraq was really a fifth-rate military power, the U.S. government exaggerated the military strength of Iraq in a propaganda campaign designed to show that Saddam Hussein is really a formidable foe; if we defeat Iraq, we have done something important. And the Bush administration makes sure that the press is not allowed to see what is happening, because they are horrified by the fact that during the Vietnam War the press began to report the atrocities we were committing. Then they decide we have to end this war quickly, so after an air campaign and a short ground campaign, the Iraqi forces crumble very quickly, and the United States declares victory.

In fact, right after the U.S. defeats Iraq, Bush says specifically in a radio address, "The specter of Vietnam has been buried forever in the desert sands of the Arabian Peninsula."[102] A wonderfully poetic statement by this president. So presumably the Vietnam syndrome is buried, which means that the American people will now accept war. I think there is some truth to this. The American people did support the Gulf War. By 1991, the Vietnam War was fifteen years behind us, and the

Howard Zinn

American people generally believed the propaganda that we had gone to war to save Kuwait.

But we were not really allowed to think about the real issues behind the American war on Iraq. We are not allowed to think about what was behind the so-called sympathy for Kuwait. We are not allowed to think about oil. When legislation giving President Bush authorization to go into Iraq was being debated in the Senate, some young people on the balcony chanted, "No blood for oil!"[103] Of course, the protesters were immediately hustled out of the Senate chamber. The American people were not supposed to think about oil as a basis for the war.

So, yes, the American people mostly believed the administration's arguments about the need to act against this tyrant Saddam Hussein, and therefore Bush had some basis for saying that the Vietnam syndrome had been buried. But I don't think it's completely true. I think there is still a memory of Vietnam in the American population, which cannot be put away. And whenever we engage in war, there always is a question: "Will this be another Vietnam?" That question does come up in the press, and people do think about it.

I think Abraham Lincoln was right. You can fool some of the people all of the time, and you can fool all of the people some of the time. But you can't fool all of the people all of the time. People in the United States woke up to what was happening to blacks in the South, and the civil rights movement became a national movement.

People woke up to what was happening in Vietnam, and we had a great national antiwar movement.

So never think that because of the polls or the news anchors, they're going to have it their way and people will always be fooled.

How important is it that Bush won?

There's hardly anything more important that people can learn about politics than that the really critical thing isn't who is sitting in the White House, but who is sitting in—in the streets, in the cafeterias, in the halls of government, in the factories. Who is protesting, who is occupying offices and demonstrating. Those are the things that determine what happens.

The Supreme Court decision in *Brown v. Board of Education*, which overthrew the "separate but equal doctrine" of segregated schools, came during the Eisenhower administration. It came with a Republican appointee as Chief Justice of the Supreme Court and with Republicans joining Democrats on the Supreme Court. And why did that happen? Was there a sudden burst of enlightenment that hit the brains of the members of the Supreme Court? Did they suddenly realize, "My God, we've misinterpreted the Fourteenth Amendment?" No. The only reason this happened in 1954 is that the world around the Supreme Court had changed.

In 1954, even though the civil rights movement hadn't

begun in earnest—it was in the next year that we had the Montgomery bus boycott and several years later that we had the sit-ins that were the heart of the movement— there were already rumblings of discontent in the South. Five different cases came up before the Supreme Court challenging segregation. *Brown v. Board of Education* was only one of the five cases.

Black people were challenging segregation in many different places in the South, and they were risking their lives to do so. The Reverend Joseph DeLaine in Clarendon County, South Carolina, was run out of town because he challenged school segregation. His church was burned, and he was declared a fugitive from justice.[104] That was typical. People went through hell, and these things were happening throughout the country. So the Brown case and the other cases wouldn't have come up before the Supreme Court if there hadn't been those acts of resistance.

At the same time, the United States was involved in the Cold War with the Soviet Union—this contest for influence in the third world, which is a nonwhite world. By 1954, it was very important for the United States to demonstrate in some way to these third-world countries that it was doing something about racial segregation. And indeed the U.S. attorneys who argued the *Brown v. Board of Education* case said the court should consider what was happening in the rest of the world and how the United States looked abroad. Attorney General Herbert Brownell asked the Supreme Court to strike down racial segregation because it "furnishes grist for the Communist propaganda mills."[105]

In other words, there are all these pressures—internal and external—that operate on the Supreme Court and on the government. It isn't simply a matter of the judges closing themselves in from the world, sitting in their chambers, and reading the words of the Constitution over and over again until something becomes clear to them. Their minds are much clarified by the things that are swirling around them in the world.

You often seem more optimistic than other writers on the left.

I think whether you're optimistic or pessimistic depends on what you're looking at. We live in a very complex society. Thousands and thousands of images come your way from television and the media. All the things that appear in the newspapers and most of the images that you see are images of "important" people. What you hear mostly in the newspapers is what the president is saying, what the secretary of state or the secretary of defense said yesterday, and so on. If you compare how much attention is paid to what government officials do compared to what ordinary people do, it's an enormous gap. So if you take seriously these images on television, and what you read in the newspapers, and take that as representative of our society, it's very disheartening. Because you're hearing

Howard Zinn

things that really confirm the status quo. You're not hearing signs of resistance to it.

But there are thousands of things that are going on all the time that aren't reported in the mainstream press and aren't reported in the major media. There's evidence of an enormous amount of energy in towns and cities all over the country—energy of people who are doing things that are noble and helpful to other people. There are thousands of organizations in this country working on issues like racial equality, women's rights, environmental protection, antimilitarism. But the work they do doesn't appear on television.

There's a counterculture. There are community newspapers and an amazing number of alternative newspapers and bookstores throughout the country. So if you're aware of that—if you pay attention to that and don't allow yourself to be overwhelmed by the images of the great and not-so-great in Washington, D.C.—you can get a sense of an enormous potential for change in this country.

A lot of people talk as if there's no alternative to the system we have now. What do you think the prospects are for class politics or for socialist politics to reach a wider audience?

I think the fall of the Soviet Union ten years ago has given us a much better opportunity to talk about socialism in a way that isn't tainted by visions of Stalinism, by a police state and the gulag. We can return to that refreshing vision of socialism that was given to us before the Soviet Union came along, by people in this country like Eugene Debs, Helen Keller, and Jack London. It's a vision of socialism that can inspire people, that inspired several million people in this country at the turn of the century. I think we have opportunities to do that.

It will take a lot of education, but it's clear that people don't have faith in government institutions. *Business Week*, which is not exactly a proletarian magazine, did a survey around a year ago, and people indicated they had very serious distrust of corporations and especially their influence over politics.[106] This skepticism shows the amount of alienation that exists, and therefore the opportunities that exist to present new ideas to people.

Bush speaks as if war is the main way in which people in this country have won their freedoms and expanded their rights.

War has always diminished our freedom. When our freedom has expanded, it has not come as a result of war or of anything the government has done but as a result of what citizens have done. The best test of that is the history of black people in the United States, the history of slavery and of segregation. It wasn't the government that initiated the movement against slavery but white and black abolitionists. It wasn't the government that initiat-

　　　　　　　　　　　　Howard Zinn

ed the battle against racial segregation in the 1950s and 1960s, but the movement of people in the South. It wasn't the government that gave the people the freedom to work eight hours a day instead of twelve hours a day. It was working people themselves who organized into unions, went out on strike, and faced the police. The government was on the other side; the government was always in support of the employers and the corporations.

The freedom of working people, the freedom of black people has always depended on the struggles of people themselves against the government. So, if we look at it historically, we certainly cannot depend on governments to maintain our liberties. We have to depend on our own organized efforts.

Another lesson of this history is that you should never depend on your legal rights. Never think you can point to a legal statute or the Constitution and say, "Look, this is what it says and therefore this is what I'm going to have." Because whatever the Constitution says and whatever the statutes say, whoever holds the power in any given situation is going to determine whether the rights you have on paper are rights you have in fact. This is a very common situation in our society. People struggled to get their legal rights, they achieved their legal rights on paper. Then the reality of power and wealth comes into play, and those legal rights don't mean very much. You have to struggle to make them real.

You are fond of quoting a question from Ignazio Silone's novel Fontamara—*a question that many people are asking now: "What are we to do?"*[107]

Yes, *"Che fare?"* was the question asked by the rebellious Italian peasants in Silone's novel. I think one thing we can do right now is to make connections to working people and support workers' rights wherever it's possible. At any given time around the country, people are engaged in labor struggles and strikes that go unreported in the press—strikes of nurses in hospitals, strikes of teachers. Too often, these are sort of set aside. People think, "These are problems for the nurses" or "These are problems for the teachers." But I think it's very important to develop the idea of solidarity, of a community solidarity, so I think that any kind of action for economic justice that can broaden the kind of interest and involve the whole community is crucial. And then we need to connect these issues, the attacks on working people here, the recession, the tax breaks for the corporations, the attacks on our civil liberties, and the wars being waged in our names and with our tax dollars.

We have a lot to do. We are all teachers, communicators. We all have contacts, we all have neighbors, we all work someplace, we can all write letters to the editor, we can organize rallies. We can engage in civil disobedience, in strikes and boycotts. We can all do what was done at other times in American history when it was necessary to build a national movement to say to the government, "No, you don't speak for us. You're not doing this for us. You aren't doing this in our name."

Bush's popularity rating is now close to 90 percent. So was Bush Sr.'s at the end of the Gulf War, but his popularity quickly collapsed and he lost the presidential election in 1991 to Clinton.

We have seen similar shifts in public opinion with all of the wars that we have fought since World War II. Certainly in the Vietnam War, we saw an absolute tidal change in public opinion. In the case of the wars that followed—notably in Grenada, Panama, the Gulf—there was an initial response to "support the president" and "support our troops." But that response changed as soon as the initial war hysteria dimmed, and as soon as people sort of woke up, looked around, and began to understand that nothing really had been accomplished and instead innocent people had been killed.

The initial support for the invasion of Panama in 1989 was based on a vague notion that we were going after Manuel Noriega because he was presumably responsible for the drug trade. It's like seeing Osama bin Laden as the one person responsible for terrorism. They focus on one person, rather than focusing on the larger problem, because the larger problem is obviously unsolvable by the methods that the government is using, whereas there is some hope that they can achieve the limited objective of finding Noriega. Of course, they found him, they jailed him, and the drug trade continued—and, in fact, increased.

So I expect that we will see a diminution—and I don't know how fast it will be—of that 90 percent support for Bush that has been paraded in the media and by the administration. I think we'll see people begin to get off that artificial high of asserting American power and declaring victory, as people begin to look around and ask, "What have we accomplished?"

I think the suppressed story of the thousands of casualties in Afghanistan is going to emerge.[108] These truths emerge eventually, despite the control of information by the major media and the government. In the United States, these tiny pockets of information exist, and they take time to reach the rest of the public; but I think there will be a moral reassessment of the issue of proportionality. People will weigh the fact that we have not really achieved our objectives—not even the limited objectives that the administration had declared—but have caused mayhem in Afghanistan. When that moral reassessment is made, I think we will see a gradual erosion of support for the administration.

What impact do you think the current economic recession will have on Bush's popularity?

The current recession has already had a very direct effect on a number of people, but this fact has been buried by the enormous attention paid to the war. As news coverage of the war recedes, though, the impact of the economic recession is going to become more and more obvious, and this will have an important result in the public's growing disaffection with the Bush administration, and maybe even disaffection with the Democratic Party, which has played such a pitifully obsequious role in this whole affair.

I think the failure of the capitalist system to solve fundamental problems will become more and more evident. At a time when the Bush administration wants an additional $48 billion for the military, funds for Medicare and Medicaid are being cut, money for education and child care is not available, and the winter has brought newspaper reports of homeless people dying in the streets and families unable to pay their heating bills. The irresponsible waste of the nation's wealth while basic needs are unmet will become clear to people.

The recent collapse of the huge Enron Corporation, leaving thousands jobless and without medical care or retirement savings, and wiping out the savings of many middle-income stockholders, is just one sign of a system that is out of control. A system that puts corporate profit above any other consideration is bound, at some point, to be exposed as a failure. I don't know when this will become clear to a large part of the American public, but it is bound to happen.

I do feel hopeful in this time that seems to lack hope, and I suppose that is based on a fundamental belief in the fact that there is a moral good sense in the American people that comes to the fore when the blanket of propaganda begins to be lifted. I think there will be a reassessment, and people who have been calling the war immoral will be vindicated at some point.

ACKNOWLEDGMENTS

Thanks to:

Dan Simon and Greg Ruggiero for seeing the political importance and timeliness of this project, and especially to Dan for his tremendously valuable editorial engagement and advice; Ahmed Shawki, editor of the *International Socialist Review*, and Alan Maass, editor of *Socialist Worker*, for encouraging us to start these interviews and for permission to reprint material published in the *ISR* and *SW* here; Arundhati Roy for speaking up; David Barsamian for showing how it should be done, in more ways than one; Martin Voelker for his invaluable help turning hours of conversations into words on the page; Michael Gallagher of Midwest Educational Graphics for the excellent maps on more than short notice; Gina Neff for her keen editorial assistance; Ashley Smith, Erik Wallenberg, and Dan Goossen for help with the Burlington, Vermont talk; Virginia Harabin, Cleve Corner, Politics and Prose Bookstore, and Jenka Soderberg for their help with the discussion on Iraq; Erik La Porta and the Media Education Foundation for their permission to use snippets of Chyng Sun's interview with Howard, filmed by Miguel Picker (mediaed.sitepassport.net); Tonja Loendorf for background materials from Alternative Radio; Nita Levison, the Rhode Island College Library, Ann Bristow at the Indiana University Library, Daniel Radosh, Joshua Cohen, and David Peterson for help with references; and Elaine Bernard and the Harvard University Trade Union Program for providing such a welcome space for our final interview.

—HOWARD ZINN AND ANTHONY ARNOVE

Additional thanks to:

My folks for teaching me early on why wars are like cyanide; my colleagues at South End Press, who made it possible for me to edit this book during a very demanding time; my comrades in the International Socialist Organization and the antiwar movement for ongoing education and collaboration; Roz and Howard for being Roz and Howard; and especially Gina, who is always on my mind.

—ANTHONY ARNOVE

APPENDIX A

EXCERPTS OF THE GENEVA PROTOCOLS

"Protocol Additional to the Geneva Conventions of 12 August 1949, and relating to the Protection of Victims of International Armed Conflicts (Protocol 1)," June 8, 1977. From Chapter II, "Civilians and Civilian Population," Article 51, "Protection of the Civilian Population":

1. The civilian population and individual civilians shall enjoy general protection against dangers arising from military operations. To give effect to this protection, the following rules, which are additional to other applicable rules of international law, shall be observed in all circumstances.

2. The civilian population as such, as well as individual civilians, shall not be the object of attack. Acts or threats of violence the primary purpose of which is to spread terror among the civilian population are prohibited.

3. Civilians shall enjoy the protection afforded by this Section, unless and for such time as they take a direct part in hostilities.

4. Indiscriminate attacks are prohibited. Indiscriminate attacks are:

(a) Those which are not directed at a specific military objective;

(b) Those which employ a method or means of combat which cannot be directed at a specific military objective; or

(c) Those which employ a method or means of combat the effects of which cannot be limited as required by this Protocol; and consequently, in each such case, are of a nature to strike military objectives and civilians or civilian objects without distinction.

5. Among others, the following types of attacks are to be considered as indiscriminate:

(a) An attack by bombardment by any methods or means which treats as a single military objective a number of clearly separated and distinct military objectives located in a city, town, village or other area containing a similar concentration of civilians or civilian objects; and

(b) An attack which may be expected to cause incidental loss of civilian life, injury to civilians, damage to civilian objects, or a combination thereof, which would be excessive in relation to the concrete and direct military advantage anticipated.

APPENDIX B

SUGGESTIONS FOR FURTHER READING

Ahmad, Eqbal. *Eqbal Ahmad: Confronting Empire.* Edited by David Barsamian. Cambridge: South End Press, 2000.

Ahmad, Eqbal. *Terrorism: Theirs and Ours.* New York: Seven Stories Press/Open Media Pamphlet Series, 2002.

Chang, Nancy. *Silencing Political Dissent: How the USA PATRIOT Act Undermines the Constitution.* New York: Seven Stories Press/Open Media Pamphlet Series, 2002.

Chomsky, Noam. *9–11.* New York: Seven Stories Press/Open Media Books, 2001.

Chomsky, Noam. *Rogue States: The Rule of Force in World Affairs.* Cambridge: South End Press, 2000.

Chomsky, Noam. *Year 501: The Conquest Continues.* Cambridge: South End Press, 1993.

Hass, Amira, *Drinking the Sea at Gaza: Days and Nights in a Land Under Siege.* Trans. Elana Wesley and Maxine Kaufman-Lacusta. New York: Henry Holt/Owl Books, 2000.

Kolko, Gabriel. *Century of War: Politics, Conflict, and Society Since 1914.* New York: New Press, 1994.

Kolko, Gabriel. *The Politics of War: The World and United States Foreign Policy, 1943–1945.* New York: Vintage, 1968.

Lens, Sidney. *The Forging of the American Empire: From the Revolution to Vietnam: A History of U.S. Imperialism.* New York: Thomas Y. Crowell Co., 1971.

Lindqvist, Sven. *A History of Bombing.* Translated by Linda Haverty Rugg. New York: New Press, 2001.

Rashid, Ahmed. *Taliban: Militant Islam, Oil, and Fundamentalism in Central Asia.* New Haven: Yale University Press/Nota Bene, 2000.

Roy, Arundhati. *Power Politics.* 2d ed. Cambridge: South End Press, 2001.

Said, Edward W. *Covering Islam: How the Media and the Experts Determine How We See the Rest of the World,* Rev. ed. New York: Vintage Books, 1997.

Shalom, Stephen R. *Imperial Alibis: Rationalizing U.S. Intervention After the Cold War.* Boston: South End Press, 1993.

Zinn, Howard. *Howard Zinn on War.* New York: Seven Stories Press, 2001.

APPENDIX C

ANTIWAR ORGANIZATIONS AND RESOURCES

ORGANIZATIONS

CENTER FOR ECONOMIC AND SOCIAL RIGHTS
162 Montague Street, 2nd floor
Brooklyn, NY 11201-3536
Phone: (718) 237-9145
Fax: (718) 237-9147
E-mail: rights@cesr.org
www.cesr.org

EDUCATION FOR PEACE IN IRAQ CENTER (EPIC)
1101 Pennsylvania Avenue SE, Suite 2
Washington, DC 20003-2229
Phone: (202) 543-6176
Fax: (202) 543-0725
E-mail: epicenter@igc.org
www.saveageneration.org

FELLOWSHIP OF RECONCILIATION
PO Box 271
Nyack, NY 10960-0271
Phone: (914) 358-4601
Fax: (914) 358-4924
E-mail: fornatl@igc.org
www.forusa.org

INTERNATIONAL SOCIALIST ORGANIZATION
PO Box 16085
Chicago, IL 60616-0085
Phone: (773) 665-9601
Fax: (773) 665-9651
E-mail: contact@internationalsocialist.org
www.internationalsocialist.org

IRAQ ACTION COALITION
7309 Haymarket Lane
Raleigh, NC 27615-5432
Phone: (919) 272-8685
Fax: (919) 846-7422
E-mail: iac@leb.net
www.iraqaction.org

PEACE ACTION
1819 H Street, NW, Suite 420
Washington, DC 20006-3603
Phone: (202) 862-9740
Fax: (202) 862-9762
E-mail: info@peace-action.org
www.peace-action.org

PHYSICIANS FOR SOCIAL RESPONSIBILITY
1101 14th Street, NW, Suite 700
Washington, DC 20005-5621
Phone: (202) 898-0150
Fax: (202) 898-0172
E-mail: psrnatl@psr.org
www.psr.org

VOICES IN THE WILDERNESS
1460 West Carmen Avenue
Chicago, IL 60640-2813
Phone: (773) 784-8065
Fax: (773) 784-8837
E-mail: kkelly@igc.org
www.vitw.org

WAR RESISTERS LEAGUE
339 Lafayette Street
New York, NY 10012-2782
Phone: (212) 228-0450
Fax: (212) 228-6193
E-mail: wrl@warresisters.org
www.warresisters.org

ALTERNATIVE INFORMATION SOURCES

ALTERNATIVE RADIO
David Barsamian
PO Box 551
Boulder, CO 80306-0551
Phone: (800) 444-1977
Fax: (303) 546-0592
E-mail: ar@orci.com
www.alternativeradio.org

FOREIGN POLICY IN FOCUS
Institute for Policy Studies
733 15th Street, NW, Suite 1020
Washington, DC 20005-2112
Phone: (202) 234-9382
Fax: (202) 387-7915
E-mail: leaverfpif@igc.org
www.foreignpolicy-infocus.org

INTERNATIONAL SOCIALIST REVIEW
PO Box 258082
Chicago, IL 60625-8082
Phone: (773) 665-7337
Fax: (773) 665-9651
E-mail: business@isreview.org
www.isreview.org

IN THESE TIMES
2040 North Milwaukee Avenue
Chicago, IL 60647-4002
Phone: (773) 772-0100
Fax: (773) 772-4180
E-mail: itt@inthesetimes.com
www.inthesetimes.org

NO WAR COLLECTIVE
www.nowarcollective.com

THE PROGRESSIVE
409 East Main Street
Madison, WI 53703-2863
Phone: (608) 257-4626
Fax: (608) 257-3373
E-mail: circ@progressive.org
www.progressive.org

SOCIALIST WORKER
PO Box 258082
Chicago, IL 60625-8082
Phone: (773) 665-7337
Fax: (773) 665-9651
E-mail: letters@socialistworker.org
www.socialistworker.org

Z MAGAZINE
18 Millfield Street
Woods Hole, MA 02543-1122
Phone: (508) 548-9063
Fax: (508) 457-0626
E-mail: lydia.sargent@zmag.org
www.zmag.org

NOTES

CHAPTER 1: 9-11

1   James P. Pinkerton, "Forget Elway—U.S. Is Throwing the Long Bomb," *Newsday* (New York), 2 February 1999, A36.

2   Eric Schmitt and James Dao, "U.S. Is Building Up Its Military Bases in Afghan Region," *New York Times*, 9 January 2002, A1; "Preparing for a Long Stay" (map), *New York Times*, 9 January 2002, A10; Elena Listvennaya, "US Unit Shows Off New Base in Kyrgyzstan," *Boston Globe*, 10 January 2002, A12.

3   Marc W. Herold, "A Dossier on Civilian Victims of United States' Aerial Bombing of Afghanistan: A Comprehensive Accounting," December 2001 (pubpages.unh.edu/~mwherold/Afghanistan.doc).

4   Doug McKinlay, "Refugees Left in the Cold at 'Slaughterhouse' Camp," *Guardian* (London), 3 January 2002, 14.

5   Robert Fisk, "Osama bin Laden: The Godfather of Terror?" *Independent*, 15 September 2001, 7.

6   Thomas L. Friedman, "U.S. Gulf Policy: Vague 'Vital Interest,'" *New York Times*, 12 August 1990, 1: 1.

7   Daniel Altman, "Diagnosis of World's Health Focuses on Economic Benefit," *New York Times*, 21 December 2001, W1.

8   Reuters, "Arthur Miller Spurns Invitation by Johnson in Vietnam Protest," *New York Times* (International edition), 28 September 1965, 2.

9   Edward R. Wolff, *Top Heavy: The Increasing Inequality of Wealth in America and What Can Be Done About It*, updated ed. (New York: New Press, 2002), 8.

10 Derrick Z. Jackson, "Toothsome Tradeoff," *Boston Globe*, 23 January 2002, A15.

11 Noam Chomsky, *9–11*, ed. Greg Ruggiero (New York: Seven Stories Press/Open Media Book, 2001), 48–49.

12 Samuel R. Berger, interview, "Hunting bin Laden," *Frontline*, PBS, 13 September 2001.

13 Howard Zinn, "Just and Unjust War," in *Howard Zinn on War* (New York: Seven Stories Press, 2001), 178.

14 Jo Thomas, "'No Sympathy' for Dead Children, McVeigh Says," *New York Times*, 29 March 2001, A12.

15 Scott Simon, "Even Pacifists Must Support This War," *Wall Street Journal*, 11 October 2001, A22.

16 Eqbal Ahmad: *Confronting Empire*, ed. David Barsamian (Cambridge: South End Press, 2000), 8; Eqbal Ahmad, *Terrorism: Theirs and Ours* (New York: Seven Stories Press/Open Media Pamphlet Series, 2001).

CHAPTER 2: SEARCHING FOR COMMON GROUND

17 James Risen, "Taliban Chiefs Prove Elusive, Americans Say," *New York Times*, 20 December 2001, B1.

18 Associated Press, "Military Response Is Not the Answer, Marchers Declare," 28 October 2001.

19 Devi Athiappan, "Peace Group Reaches Out to Shoppers," *Newsday* (New York), 17 December 2001, A13.

20   Richard Falk, "Ends and Means: Defining a Just War," *The Nation* 273, no. 13 (29 October 2001): 11–15. Falk later modified his views partially, writing, "With each passing day, my assessment shifts to reach the conclusion that the United States is waging an unjust war in Afghanistan, and it is doing so in a manner that is likely to have severe blowback consequences." See Falk, "Falk Replies," *The Nation* 273, no. 17 (26 November 2001): 60–61, and Howard Zinn, Letter to the Editor, *The Nation* 273, no. 17 (26 November 2001): 2. However, Falk later wrote that the "rapid collapse of the Taliban regime" had given him "a restored sense of proportionality between means and ends." See Falk, "In Defense of 'Just War' Thinking," *The Nation* 273, no. 21 (24 December 2001): 23.

21   Janny Scott, "Closing a Scrapbook Full of Life and Sorrow," *New York Times*, 31 December 2001, B6.

22   Carla Baranauckas et al., "The Victims," *New York Times*, 31 December 2001, B6.

23   Rebecca Blumenstein, "Many Relatives of Victims Feel Uneasy, Fear Innocent Will Die in Retaliation," *Wall Street Journal*, 8 October 2001, A8; Letter to the Editor, "Out of the Horror, a Test of Humanity," *New York Times*, 4 January 2002, A20; Jim Rutenberg, "A Handful of the Bereaved Become Advocates for All," *New York Times*, 29 December 2001, B1.

24   Fairness and Accuracy in Reporting, "Incomplete Portrait," *Extra!* 15, no. 1 (January–February 2002): 5; "Corrections," *New York Times*, 9 December 2001, 1: A2.

25   Mark Landler, "Sharing Grief to Find Understanding," *New York Times*, 17 January 2002, A16.

26   Pam Belluck, "New Wave of the Homeless Floods Cities' Shelters," *New York Times*, 18 December 2001, A11.

27 Jim Drinkard, "House OKs $100B for Economy," *USA Today,* 25 October 2001, 5A.

28 Seymour Melman, *After Capitalism: From Managerialism to Workplace Democracy* (New York: Knopf, 2001).

29 Peter Novick, *The Holocaust in American Life* (Boston: Mariner Books/Houghton Mifflin, 2000), 221.

30 Anthony Lewis, "Dust in Our Eyes," *New York Times,* 4 December 2001, A21. The Uniting and Strengthening America by Providing Appropriate Tools Required to Intercept and Obstruct Terrorism Act was signed by Bush on 26 October 2001. Adam Clymer, "Bush Quickly Signs Measure Aiding Antiterrorism Effort," *New York Times,* 27 October 2001, B5.

31 Nancy Chang and the Center for Constitutional Rights, *The Silencing of Political Dissent: How the USA PATRIOT Act Undermines the Constitution* (New York: Seven Stories Press/Open Media Pamphlet Series, 2001); Tim Weiner, "The C.I.A. Widens Its Domestic Reach," *New York Times,* 20 January 2002, 4: 1; Linda Greenhouse, "In New York Visit, O'Connor Foresees Limits on Freedoms," *New York Times,* 29 September 2001, B5.

32 Nancy Chang, *Silencing of Political Dissent,* 3–4.

33 Helen Dewar, "President to Sign Defense Bill," *Washington Post,* 15 December 2001, A7; Mark Mazzetti, "How to Fight in the Future," *The Economist,* special issue, *The World in 2002,* 56.

34 James Dao, "Reprieve for Pentagon Budget," *New York Times,* 25 January 2002, A18.

35 Jacob M. Schlesinger, "As Budget Deficits Loom, Many Promises, Programs Could Suffer," *Wall Street Journal,* 24 January 2002, A1; Robert Pear and Robin Toner, "Grim

Choices Face States in Making Cuts in Medicaid," *New York Times*, 14 January 2002, A1.

36   Editorial, "Aid for the Poor," *Financial Times* (London), 19 July 2001, 20.

37   John Donnelly, "US Urged to Fund AIDS War in Africa," *Boston Globe*, 16 March 2001, A1.

38   Editorial, "Mr. Bush's New Gravitas," *New York Times*, 12 October 2001, A24.

39   Jerry L. Martin and Anne D. Neal, *Defending Civilization: How Our Universities Are Failing America and What Can Be Done About It* (Washington, D.C.: ACTA, 2001), 3 (online at www.goacta.org/Reports/defciv.pdf); Emily Eakin, "On the Lookout for Patriotic Incorrectness," *New York Times*, 24 November 2001, A15.

40   John Ashcroft, "Excerpts From Attorney General's Testimony Before Senate Judiciary Committee," *New York Times*, 7 December 2001, B6.

41   Martin and Neal, *Defending Civilization*, 10; Eakin, "Patriotic Incorrectness," A15.

42   David J. Garrrow, *The FBI and Martin Luther King, Jr.: From "Solo" to Memphis* (New York: W. W. Norton, 1981), 49.

CHAPTER 3: A PEACEFUL NATION?

43   George Bush, "Bush's Remarks on U.S. Military Strikes in Afghanistan," *New York Times*, 8 October 2001, B6.

44   Vincent Jauvert, interview with Zbigniew Brzezinski, "Oui, la CIA est entrée en Afghanistan avant les Russes...," *Nouvel Observateur* (France) 1732 (January 1998) (archives.nouvelobs.com/).

45   John Kifner, "Forget the Past: It's A War Unlike Any Other," *New York Times*, 23 September 2001, 4: 8.

46   Eduardo Galeano, *Upside Down: A Primer for the Looking-Glass World*, trans. Mark Fried (New York: Picador USA, 2001), 195.

47   SOA Watch (www.soaw.org); Frida Berrigan, "Beyond the School of the Americas: U.S. Military Training Programs Here and Abroad," Arms Trade Research Center, World Policy Institute, May 2000; Dana Priest, "U.S. Instructed Latins on Executions, Torture; Manuals Used 1982–91, Pentagon Reveals," *Washington Post*, 21 September 1996, A1; Tina Rosenberg, "Another Hallowed Terror Ground," *New York Times Magazine*, 13 January 2002, 6: 26.

48   Henry A. Kissinger, "The Pitfalls of Universal Jurisdiction," *Foreign Affairs* 80, no. 4 (July/August 2001): 86.

CHAPTER 4: THE NEED FOR DISSENT

49   President George W. Bush, Address to Joint Session of Congress, "September 11, 2001, Terrorist Attacks on the United States," Federal News Service, 20 September 2001.

50   Andrew Sullivan, "America at War: America Wakes Up to a World of Fear," *Sunday Times* (London), 16 September 2001.

51   Richard L. Berke, "Bush 'Is My Commander,' Gore Declares in Call for Unity," *New York Times*, 30 September 2001, 1: 29.

52   Jim Rutenberg and Bill Carter, "Draping Newscasts With the Flag," *New York Times*, 20 September 2001, C8; Dan Rather, interview by Larry King, "America's New War: Healing the Wound in America's Heart," *Larry King Live*, CNN, 4 October 2001.

53 Ed Hayward, "High School Speech by Peace Prof. Raises Ire," *Boston Herald*, 20 November 2001, 7.

54 Howard Zinn, *A People's History of the United States: 1492–Present* (New York: HarperCollins, 1999).

55 *Newton Tab*, 5 December 2001, 8–11.

56 Fareed Zakaria, "The Politics of Rage: Why Do They Hate Us?" *Newsweek*, 15 October 2001, 22.

57 Ahmed Rashid, *Taliban: Militant Islam, Oil, and Fundamentalism in Central Asia* (New Haven: Yale University Press/Nota Bene, 2000).

58 Stephen R. Shalom, *Imperial Alibis: Rationalizing U.S. Intervention After the Cold War* (Boston: South End Press, 1993).

59 John Reed, "Whose War?" (1917), in *Shaking the World: John Reed's Revolutionary Journalism*, ed. John Newsinger (Chicago: Bookmarks, 1998), 93.

60 David McCullough, *John Adams* (New York: Simon and Schuster, 2001).

61 The Espionage Act, H.R. 291, 65th Cong., 1st sess., ch. 30 (15 June 1917).

62 Frederick Douglass, "The Meaning of July Fourth for the Negro," in *Frederick Douglass: Selected Speeches and Writings*, ed. Philip S. Foner (Chicago: Lawrence Hill Books, 1999), 190.

63 Elisabeth Bumiller, "Military Tribunals Needed in Difficult Time, Bush Says," *New York Times*, 20 November 2001, B5; William Safire, "Seizing Dictatorial Power," *New York Times*, 15 November 2001, A31.

64 Elisabeth Bumiller, "Putting Name to Bush Justice Dept.: Kennedy," *New York Times*, 21 November 2001, A14.

65   Safire, "Seizing Dictatorial Power," A31.

66   Elisabeth Bumiller, "Bush Keeps a Grip on Presidential Papers," *New York Times*, 2 November 2001, A22.

67   Alan Duke, "Doubts Plagued LBJ on Vietnam Early in the War," CNN, 15 February 1997; Michael R. Beschloss, *Reaching for Glory: Lyndon Johnson's Secret White House Tapes, 1964–1965* (New York: Simon and Schuster, 2001).

68   David E. Sanger, "New Tapes Indicate Johnson Doubted Attack in Tonkin Gulf," *New York Times*, 6 November 2001, A18.

CHAPTER 5: WAR ON CIVILIANS

69   Gabriel Kolko, *Century of War: Politics, Conflict, and Society Since 1914* (New York: New Press, 1994), 470; Randall Forsberg, Jonathan Dean, and Saul Mendlovitz, "Global Action to Prevent War," *Boston Review* 24, no. 1 (February–March 1999): 4.

70   Sven Lindqvist, *A History of Bombing*, trans. Linda Haverty Rugg (New York: New Press, 2001), 5.

71   Lindqvist, *History of Bombing*, 83–104.

72   Lindqvist, *History of Bombing*, 91.

73   Lindqvist, *History of Bombing*, 107.

74   Alfonso A. Narvaez, "Gen. Curtis LeMay, an Architect of Strategic Air Power, Dies at 83," *New York Times*, 2 October 1990, B6.

75   Barton Gellman, "U.S. Bombs Missed 70% of Time," *Washington Post*, 16 March 1991, A1.

76   Barton Gellman, "Allied Air War Struck Broadly in Iraq," *Washington Post*, 23 June 1991, A1; Gellman, "U.S. Bombs Missed," A1.

77   Kirk Johnson, "Afghan Caves, an Egyptian Courtroom and the Trade Center Toll," *New York Times*, 21 November 2001, B1; Elizabeth Becker and Eric Schmitt, "U.S. Planes Bomb a Red Cross Site," *New York Times*, 27 October 2001, A1.

78   Indira A. R. Lakshmanan, "UN's Peaceful Mission Loses 4 to War," *Boston Globe*, 10 October 2001, A1.

79   Tim Wiener, "U.S. Bombs Hit 3 Towns, Afghans Say," *New York Times*, 2 December 2001, B2; Tim Wiener, "Villagers Yearn for the Old, Eternal Afghanistan," *New York Times*, 3 December 2001, B5.

80   David Shaw, "Media Under Public Barrage Over Content of War Coverage," *Los Angeles Times*, 18 November 2001, A8; Gay Alcorn, "News of Afghan Dead Is Buried," *The Age* (Melbourne), 12 January 2002, 17.

81   Jim Mannion, "Pentagon Acknowledges Bomb Went Astray in Kabul, Herat," Agence France-Presse, 24 October 2001.

82   Carol Morello, "Tight Control Marks Coverage of Afghan War," *Washington Post*, 7 December 2001, A43; Patrick E. Tyler, "Powell Says U.S. Will Stay in Iraq 'For Some Months to Come,'" *New York Times*, 23 March 1991, 1: 1.

83   Said Mohammad Azam, "UN Says US Bombs Struck Mosque, Village as Civilian Casualties Mount," Agence France-Presse, 25 October 2001.

84   John Donnelly, "Unintended Victims Fill Afghan Hospital," *Boston Globe*, 5 December 2001, A1.

85   Barry Bearak, "In Village Where Civilians Died, Anger Cannot Be Buried," *New York Times*, 16 December 2001, 1: B3.

86   Morello, "Tight Control," A43; Michael R. Gordon, "Military Is Putting Heavier Limits on Reporters' Access," *New York Times*, 21 October 2001, 1: B3.

87   Jules Crittenden, "'Air Supremacy' Achieved," *Boston Herald*, 10 October 2001, 3.

88   Howard Zinn, "One Iraqi's Story," in *Iraq Under Siege: The Deadly Impact of Sanctions and War*, ed. Anthony Arnove (Cambridge: South End Press, 2000), 105.

89   Jeff Cohen and Norman Solomon, "Smithsonian Bows to Media Onslaught," *Seattle Times*, 14 February 1995, B5; Anthony Shadid, "Bombed Village Is Testimony to Risks to Civilians," *Boston Globe*, 10 January 2002, A1.

CHAPTER 6: THE LOGIC OF WAR

90   Mark Binelli et al., "Howard Zinn," *Rolling Stone*, 30 December 1999–6 January 2000, 66. Bob Dylan, "Masters of War," in *Lyrics, 1962–1985* (New York: Knopf, 1985), 56.

91   Dylan, "George Jackson," *Lyrics*, 302; Dylan and Jacques Levy, "Hurricane," *Lyrics*, 375–77; Dylan, "The Death of Emmett Till," *Lyrics*, 20.

92   Dylan, "Blowin' in the Wind," *Lyrics*, 53; Dylan, "John Brown," *Lyrics*, 46–47.

93   Dylan, "With God on Our Side," *Lyrics*, 93.

94   Ronald Reagan, "Thanksgiving Day, 1986," *Christian Science Monitor*, 14 November 1986, 6.

95   Kenneth R. Bazinet, "A Fight Vs. Evil, Bush and Cabinet Tell U.S.," *Daily News* (New York), 17 September 2001, 8.

96 Eugene Debs, "EVD to *New York Sun*," (29 November 1915), in *Letters of Eugene V. Debs, Vol. 2: 1913–1919*, ed. J. Roberts Constantine (Urbana: University of Illinois Press, 1990), 205.

97 Dwight D. Eisenhower, "The Chance for Peace," speech to the American Society of Newspaper Editors, Washington D.C., 16 April 1953.

98 Rosa Luxemburg, "Peace Utopias," in *Rosa Luxemburg Speaks*, ed. Mary-Alice Waters (New York: Pathfinder, 1970), 251.

CHAPTER 7: NOT IN OUR NAME

99 Mark Twain, "The War Prayer," in *Mark Twain on the Damned Human Race*, ed. Janet Smith (New York: Hill and Wang, 1994), 67; Helen Scott, "The Mark Twain They Didn't Teach Us About in School," *International Socialist Review* 10 (Winter 2000): 61–65.

100 R. W. Apple, Jr., "A Military Quagmire Remembered: Afghanistan as Vietnam," *New York Times*, 31 October 2001, B1; John M. Anspacher, "U.S. 'Advisers': A Tale of Saigon," *New York Times*, 2 November 2001, A24; Michael R. Gordon and Steven Lee Myers, "U.S. Will Increase Number of Advisers in Afghanistan," *New York Times*, 1 November 2001, A1; James Brooke, "Unease Grows in Philippines on U.S. Forces," *New York Times*, 19 January 2002, A1; Editorial, "Chasing Abu Sayyaf," *Boston Globe*, 25 January 2002, A22.

101 Zinn, *A People's History of the United States*, 539–40.

102 Peter Applebome, "War Heals Wounds at Home, But Not All," *New York Times*, 4 March 1991, A1.

103 Peter Jennings, *World News Tonight*, ABC, 11 January 1991.

104 Howard Zinn, *Declarations of Independence: Cross-Examining American Ideology* (New York: HarperPerennial, 1991), 242.

105 John Hope Franklin and Alfred A. Moss, Jr., *From Slavery to Freedom: A History of African Americans*, 7th ed. (New York: McGraw-Hill, 1994), 412; Mary L. Dudziak, *Cold War Civil Rights: Race and the Image of American Democracy* (Princeton: Princeton University Press, 2000), 131.

106 Aaron Bernstein, "Too Much Corporate Power?" *Business Week* 3698 (11 September 2000): 144.

107 Ignazio Silone, *Fontamara*, trans. Gwenda David and Eric Mosbacher (London: Red Words, 1994), 177.

108 Seumas Milne, "The Innocent Dead in a Coward's War: Estimates Suggest US Bombs Have Killed at Least 3,767 Civilians," *Guardian* (London), 20 December 2001, 16; Herold, "A Dossier on Civilian Victims."

INDEX

Abolition, 70, 72, 114

Abu Sayyaf, 106

Adams, John, 67

Afghanistan, 6 *map*
   "advisers" in, 105
   Camp Rhino in, 88
   continuation of war in, 29
   deaths in, 11, 21, 33
   failure of objectives in, 27, 28
   harm from bombing in, 11
   human tragedies in, 34
   information on, 65
   Russia in, 51
   smart bombs in, 82–88
   Taliban in, 27, 51
   United States support for
      mujahedeen in, 51

After Capitalism (Melman), 38

Agence France-Presse, 86

Ahmad, Eqbal, 26

Aid for Families with Dependent
   Children, 37

AIDS, 43–44

Alien and Sedition Acts (1798),
   66, 67

American Council of Trustees
   and Alumni, 46

Amnesty International, 64

Anaconda Copper, 49

Anarchism, 70

Anti-Americanism, 41–42

Anti-Ballistic Missile Treaty, 64, 96

Anti-Imperialist League, 100–101

Antiwar movement, 99–100
   as "anti-American," 41–42
   current, 36, 104
   decentralization of, 29–30
   demonstrations and, 30
   media reports on, 30
   tactics of, 38
   weakness of, 29–30

Arms race, 96

Ashcroft, John, 45, 46

Barsamian, David, 26

Bearak, Barry, 87

Berger, Samuel R. "Sandy," 21

Berkman, Alexander, 69

bin Laden, Osama, 13, 17, 27, 34,
   52, 117

Blacklisting, 47

"Blowin' in the Wind" (song), 92

Bombings
   in Afghanistan, 11, 50, 52,
      82–88
   in Cambodia, 50
   car, 26
   decisions on, 28
   effect on terrorism, 21
   as form of terrorism, 33
   in Germany, 78, 80, 102

human side of, 88–90
indiscriminate, 44–45
information on, 32
insecurity and, 18
in Japan, 78, 102
in Laos, 50
military targets and, 33
pinpoint, 82, 83
precision, 81
psychological impact of, 82
in Sudan, 52
World War II, 80
in Yugoslavia, 24, 52
Boston Globe, 83, 86, 106
Boycotts, 116
Brownell, Herbert, 111–112
Brown v. Board of Education,
    110–112
Brzezinski, Zbigniew, 51
Bush, George H. W.
    attempt to undo "Vietnam syn-
        drome," 108
    in Gulf War, 52
    Panama and, 52
    popularity rating, 117
Bush, George W.
    access to presidential papers
        and, 74–76
    calls for support for, 57, 58
    claims on making world safer,
        27–29
    claims the United States is
        "peaceful," 50–52
    on deportations without trial, 48
    impact of recession on,
        118–119

military tribunals and, 72–73
popularity rating, 117
positive media coverage of,
    44–45
support for, 117–118
suspension of civil liberties by,
    40
on terrorism targets, 12–13
use of war as cover for worsen-
    ing conditions, 37
Cambodia, 50, 106, 107
Camp Rhino, 88
Capitalism
    failure of, 119
    state and, 97
    war and, 97–98
Carter, Jimmy, 51
Center for Constitutional Rights,
    40
Center for Defense Information, 64
Center for Economic and Social
    Rights, 127
Central America, 51
Century of War (Kolko), 78
Chang, Nancy, 40
Cheney, Lynne, 45–47
Chile
    overthrow of government in, 49
    United States corporations in, 49
Chomsky, Noam, 45, 61, 65
Christophe, Charles, 35
Churchill, Winston, 80
CIA, 40, 55
Civil disobedience, 23, 116
    Pentagon Papers as, 103

Civil liberties. *See also* Freedom
     of speech
  attacks on, 38–40, 45
  curtailment of, 66
  governmental control of, 66
  immigrants and, 39
  terrorism as rationale for sup-
       pression of, 48
  willingness to restrict, 39
Civil rights movement, 109–112
Civil War
  antiwar sentiment in, 100
  draft riots in, 100
Clarke, Victoria, 85
Class issues, 37, 100
Clinton, Bill, 10, 21, 52, 89, 117
CNN (television), 85
Cold War, 47, 48
Collateral damage, 24, 82, 85
Colonialism, 14, 102
Communism, 22, 47, 48, 49
Compassion, 32
Concentration camps, 48, 78
Constitution, 58
  First Amendment to, 47, 68
Corporations
  benefits given to, 37
  enrichment of, 37
  hostility toward, 42
  missile defense and, 96
  in Saudi Arabia, 14
  tax cuts for, 18–19
  war profits by, 28
  weapons production and, 97–98
Costa Rica
  military interventions in, 51

Counterculture, 113
Counterterrorism, 26
Cuomo, Kerry Kennedy, 73
D'Aubuisson, Roberto, 55
Deaths
  in Afghanistan, 11, 21, 33
  in Central America, 48
  civilian, 11, 24, 33, 78, 80, 84–90
  in refugee camps, 11
  in Southeast Asia, 48
  in Sudan, 21
  technology and, 22, 79
Debs, Eugene, 68, 94, 95, 114
Declaration of Independence, 71
Defense Science Board, 9
DeLaine, Joseph, 111
Denmark, 23
Deportations, 47–48, 67, 69
DiFranco, Ani, 93
Dissent
  Douglass on, 70–72
  information on, 63–65
  intolerance for, 66
  need for, 57–77
  security precautions and, 62
  stifling, 65, 66
  teach-ins on, 63–65
  variability of, 71
Dominican Republic
  military interventions in, 51
Douglass, Frederick, 70–72
Draft riots, 100
Due process, 67
Dylan, Bob, 92, 93
East Timor, 51
Education, 60–61

Education for Peace in Iraq Center, 127
Eisenhower, Dwight, 96, 110
El Mozote, 55
El Salvador, 55
  military interventions in, 51
England, 14
Enron Corporation, 119
Espionage Act, 67, 68
"Even Pacifists Must Support This War" (Simon), 25
Falk, Richard, 31, 134n20
Fanaticism, 16
Fascism, 22, 23, 102
FBI, 46
  "Reserve Index" and, 48
Fellowship of Reconciliation, 127
Fifth column, 57
Fisk, Robert, 13
Fontamara (Silone), 116
Ford, Gerald, 107
Foreign aid, 43
Foreign policy, 13, 16, 17, 54, 66
  criticisms of, 61–63
  overview on, 65
Foreign Policy in Focus (journal), 129
France, 14
Freedom of Information Act, 74
Freedom of speech, 61–63, 65–70
Friedman, Thomas, 14
Friendly fire, 88
Frontline (television), 21
Galeano, Eduardo, 54
Garrow, David, 48
Gellman, Barton, 82

Geneva Conventions, 79, 123–124
Germany, 23, 78, 80, 102
Global Exchange, 36
Goldman, Emma, 69
Gore, Al, 58
Government
  as artificial entity, 71
  calls for support for, 57–58
  control of civil liberties by, 66
  as counterrevolutionary force, 71
  criticism of, 57, 62
  deception by, 62, 63, 77
  lack of faith in, 114
  reasons to distrust, 75
Grenada, 107
Guatemala
  overthrow of government in, 49, 51
  United States corporations in, 49
Gulf of Tonkin incident, 76–77
Gulf War, 14, 24, 63, 108
  antiwar movement during, 29
Haiti, 71–72
Harris, Arthur, 80, 81
Health care
  cuts in, 20, 119
  funding for, 18
Herold, Marc, 11
A History of Bombing (Lindqvist), 80, 81
Hitchens, Christopher, 45
Hitler, Adolf, 20, 23, 102
Homelessness, 37
Honduras
  military interventions in, 51

Hussein, Saddam, 89, 108, 109
Ibn Saud (King of Saudi Arabia), 14
Immigrants, 39, 66
Imperial Alibis (Shalom), 65
Imperialism, 23, 97, 101
Indonesia, 51
Industrial Workers of the World, 67
Internal Security Act (1950), 48
International Socialist
    Organization, 128
International Socialist Review
    (magazine), 65, 130
In These Times (journal), 130
Iran
    overthrow of government in, 51
Iraq, 13, 14–15, 82, 89, 91, 109
    possible military action
        against, 28, 29
    sanctions on, 17
Iraq Action Coalition, 128
Isaacson, Walter, 85
Isolationism, 102
Israel, 13, 17, 26
Jackson, Jesse, 46
Jackson, Kenneth, 33
Japan, 15, 78, 91, 102
Jefferson, Thomas, 71–72
"John Brown" (song), 92
Johnson, Lyndon, 19, 75, 76, 77
"Just and Unjust War" (Zinn), 22
Keller, Helen, 114
Kennedy, John F., 75
Kennedy, Robert F., 73
King, Martin Luther, Jr., 25, 48, 103
Kissinger, Henry, 55, 56, 107
Kolko, Gabriel, 78

Korean War, 50
    civilian deaths in, 79
Kosovo, 24
Kuwait, 109
    military interventions in, 52
Laos, 50
Lapan, Dave, 91
Larry King Live (television), 58
Lasar, Rita, 36–37
Late Show with David Letterman
    (television), 58
Lee, Barbara, 54
LeMay, Curtis, 81
Lewis, Anthony, 40
Lincoln, Abraham, 109
Lindqvist, Sven, 80, 81
London, Jack, 114
Luxemburg, Rosa, 97
McCarran-Walter Immigration
    Act (1952), 47–48
McNamara, Robert, 77
McVeigh, Timothy, 24
The Masses (magazine), 68
"Masters of War" (song), 92
Mayaguez affair, 106–107
Mecca, 17
Media
    alternative, 64, 113
    on antiwar sentiment, 41–42
    complicity in government
        deception, 62
    control of, 11
    reporting of war atrocities, 108
    restrictions on, 87–88
    withholding stories from pub-
        lic, 85–88

Melman, Seymour, 38
Mexican War, 53, 63, 99
  antiwar sentiment in, 99
  San Patricio Battalion in, 99
Middle East
  United States interests in,
    14–15
  United States policies in, 64
Militarism, 23, 97
Military bases, 7 *map*
Military expenditures
  alternative uses for, 18
  effect on terrorism, 9
  "guns and butter" issues and,
    42–44
  increases in, 18, 20, 43
  on National Missile Defense
    program, 42, 43
Military interventions
  Afghanistan, 21, 51
  Caribbean, 50
  Central America, 51
  Costa Rica, 51
  Dominican Republic, 51
  El Salvador, 51
  Grenada, 107
  Guatemala, 50, 51
  Honduras, 51
  hostility toward, 42
  Iran, 51
  limited, 31, 44
  need for cessation of, 9
  Nicaragua, 51
  Panama, 117
  Philippines, 107
  Saudi Arabia, 13

  as solution to attacks of
    September 11, 9–10
  Sudan, 21
  terrorism as rationale for, 48
  to undo "Vietnam syndrome,"
    108
  by United States, 50–52
  Yugoslavia, 24
Military tribunals, 39–40, 72–73,
  74
Miller, Arthur, 19
Milosevic, Slobodan, 24
Movements
  antiwar, 29, 30, 41–42, 99–100
  civil rights, 109–112
  internal, 99
  underground, 23
Mussolini, Benito, 23, 102
National Missile Defense pro-
  gram, 42, 43, 95–96
National Public Radio, 25
The Nation (magazine), 31
New Republic (magazine), 57
New York Times, 14, 27, 32, 36,
  37, 40, 43, 44, 52, 58, 64, 74,
  76, 83, 105
Nicaragua
  Contras in, 51
  military interventions in, 51
Niemöller, Martin, 39
Nixon, Richard, 46, 75, 76
Noriega, Manuel, 55, 117, 118
Norway, 23
Nuclear
  proliferation, 64
  weapons, 31, 102

O'Connor, Sandra Day, 40
Oil, 14–15
Pacifism, 25, 99–100, 102
Palestine, 17, 26
Palmer, A. Mitchell, 69
Palmer raids, 69
Panama, 52, 117
Patriotism, 38
Peace Action, 128
Pentagon
    estimates of civilian deaths by, 11
    news releases from, 85
    request for increases in budget, 43
Pentagon Papers, 103
A People's History of the United States (Zinn), 60
Philippines War, 63
    antiwar sentiment in, 100–101
Physicians for Social Responsibility, 128
Polk, James, 53
"Portraits in Grief" (*New York Times*), 33, 34
Potorti, David, 35, 36
Powell, Colin, 85–86
Principle of proportionality, 79
The Progressive (magazine), 130
al-Obaidi, Mohammad, 88–90
al-Qaeda, 12, 27, 34
Racism, 23, 102
Rashid, Ahmed, 65
Rather, Dan, 58
Reagan, Ronald, 10, 43, 51, 94, 107

Recession, 20
    "guns and butter" issues and, 42–44
    impact on Bush, 118–119
Reed, John, 65, 67
Refugees, 11, 24
Resistance
    popular, 24
    through music, 93
    without war, 23
Revolutionary War, 99
    antiwar sentiment in, 99
Riots
    draft, 100
    ghetto, 103
Rodriguez, Orlando and Phyllis, 35
Rolling Stone (magazine), 92
Roosevelt, Franklin D., 14
Roosevelt, Theodore, 69
Rumsfeld, Donald, 88
Rusk, Dean, 77
Russell, Richard, 75
Sacco, Nicola, 70
Safire, William, 74
Said, Amin, 37
Sanders, Bernie, 54
San Patricio Battalion, 99
Saudi Arabia, 13
    military troops in, 17, 52
    United States control in, 28
    United States corporations in, 14
School of the Americas, 54, 55
Sedition Act, 67, 68
Seeger, Pete, 93
Segregation, 110–112, 114, 115
Senate Judiciary Committee, 46

September 11 attacks
    analogies to Pearl Harbor and, 20
    lessons from, 15–18
    military solution to, 9–10
Shalom, Stephen, 65
Shays Rebellion, 71
Silone, Ignazio, 116
Simon, Scott, 25
Slavery, 71, 72, 100, 114
Socialism, 113–114
Socialist Party, 67
Socialist Worker (magazine), 130
Socialist Workers Party, 22
Sontag, Susan, 61
Spanish-American War, 53, 63
    antiwar sentiment in, 100–101
Spanish Civil War, 57
Springsteen, Bruce, 93
Stone, I.F., 63
Strikes, 23, 116
Sudan, 21, 52
Sullivan, Andrew, 57
Swift, Jane, 20
Taliban, 27, 51, 134n20
Taliban (Rashid), 65
Tang Island, 107
Terrorism
    actions against, 10–12
    broader definition of, 16
    common ground on, 27–49
    domestic, 24
    effect of bombings on, 21
    effect of military expenditures
        on, 9
    evaluating, 25–26
    of governments, 16
    immorality of, 60
    international experience of, 10,
        16, 41
    military responses to, 20–21
    provocation of, 21
    as rationale for militarization, 48
    reasons for, 12, 13
    religious symbolism and, 13
    response to, 60
    as response to terrorism, 12
    revenge and, 35, 36
    roots of, 61
    safety from, 18
    of sects, 16
    solutions to, 26
    United States policy and, 16, 17
Treason, 57
Truman, Harry, 91
Turkey
    United States control in, 28
Twain, Mark, 100–101
United Fruit Company, 49
United States
    corporate international
        interests, 14
    economic stimulus package in,
        37–38
    foreign policy, 13, 16, 17, 54
    interests in Middle East, 14–15
    international image of, 17, 54
    military involvements by,
        50–52
    opposition to International
        War Crimes Tribunal, 55–56
    policy in Israel, 17

unmet needs in, 19, 37, 42–44,
    119
United States Special Forces, 106
United States Strategic Air
    Command, 81
United States Supreme Court,
    110–112
USA PATRIOT Act, 39–40
U.S.S. *Maddox*, 76–77
U.S.S. *Maine*, 53, 100–101
Vanzetti, Bartolomeo, 70
Vietnam syndrome, 104–110
Vietnam Veterans Against the
    War, 103
Vietnam War, 50, 51, 63
    antiwar sentiment in, 29,
        102–104
    civilian deaths in, 78–79
    Gulf of Tonkin incident in,
        76–77
Voices in the Wilderness, 129
Wall Street Journal, 25, 35, 43, 64
War
    capitalism and, 97–98
    on civilians, 78–91
    as crusade, 94
    economic systems and, 38
    effect on needs of population,
        19–20, 37, 42–44
    hysteria over, 70
    of independence, 71
    inevitability of, 38
    invoking God in, 93–94
    just and unjust, 22–25, 31, 79,
        134*n20*
    logic of, 92–98

oil and, 14, 15
    perpetual, 28
    technology and, 22, 23, 79
    uncertainty about, 31
War crimes tribunal, 55–56
War on terrorism
    human tragedies in, 33, 34
    public support for, 12, 44–45
"The War Prayer" (Twain), 101
War Resisters League, 129
Washington Post, 82, 85, 87
Western Hemisphere Institute for
    Security Cooperation, 54, 55
Wilson, Woodrow, 68–69
"With God on Our Side" (song), 93
Wolff, Edward, 19–20
World Health Organization, 18
World War I, 63
    antiwar sentiment in, 101–102
    Socialist Party and, 67
World War II
    antiwar sentiment in, 101–102
    bombings in, 78, 80
    nuclear weapons in, 31
    Pearl Harbor analogies and, 20
Yugoslavia, 24

BOOKS BY HOWARD ZINN

Emma. Cambridge: South End Press, 2002.

Three Strikes: Miners, Musicians, Salesgirls, and the Fighting Spirit of Labor's Last Century, with Dana Frank and Robin D. G. Kelley. Boston: Beacon Press, 2001.

Howard Zinn on War. New York: Seven Stories Press, 2001.

Howard Zinn on History. New York: Seven Stories Press, 2001.

La otra historia de los Estados Unidos. New York: Seven Stories Press, 2001.

Marx in Soho: A Play on History. Cambridge: South End Press, 1999.

The Future of History: Interviews with David Barsamian. Monroe, Maine: Common Courage Press, 1999.

A People's History of the United States: 1492–Present, Twentieth Anniversary Edition. New York: HarperCollins, 1999.

The Zinn Reader: Writings on Disobedience and Democracy. New York: Seven Stories Press, 1997.

You Can't Be Neutral on a Moving Train: A Personal History of Our Times. Boston: Beacon Press, 1994.

Failure to Quit: Reflections of an Optimistic Historian. Monroe, Maine: Common Courage Press, 1993.

Declarations of Independence: Cross-Examining American Ideology. New York: HarperCollins, 1990.

The Politics of History, 2d ed. Urbana: University of Illinois Press, 1990.

Justice: Eyewitness Accounts. Boston: Beacon Press, 1977.

Postwar America: 1945–1971. Indianapolis: Bobbs-Merrill, 1973.

Disobedience and Democracy: Nine Fallacies of Law and Order. New York: Vintage Books, 1968.

Vietnam: The Logic of Withdrawal. Boston: Beacon Press, 1967.

SNCC: The New Abolitionists. Boston: Beacon Press, 1964.

The Southern Mystique. New York: Knopf, 1964.

LaGuardia in Congress. Ithaca: Cornell University Press, 1959.

Howard Zinn

ABOUT THE AUTHOR

Howard Zinn is professor emeritus at Boston University. He is the author of the classic *A People's History of the United States*, "a brilliant and moving history of the American people from the point of view of those...whose plight has been largely omitted from most histories" (*Library Journal*). A television adaptation of *A People's History of the United States* is currently being co-produced by Matt Damon, Ben Affleck, and Chris Moore for HBO. Zinn has received the Lannan Foundation Literary Award for Nonfiction and the Eugene V. Debs award for his writing and political activism.

Zinn is the author of numerous books, including *The Zinn Reader*, the autobiographical *You Can't Be Neutral on a Moving Train*, and the play *Marx in Soho*.

Zinn grew up in Brooklyn and worked in the shipyards before serving as an air force bombardier in World War II. Zinn was chair of the history department at Spelman College, where he actively participated in the civil rights movement, before taking a position at Boston University. He now lives with his wife, Roslyn, in Massachusetts and lectures widely on history and contemporary politics.

ABOUT THE EDITOR

Anthony Arnove is an editor and publisher at South End Press in Cambridge, Massachusetts. He is the editor of *Iraq Under Siege: The Deadly Impact of Sanctions and War* (Cambridge: South End Press; London: Pluto Press, 2000). His writing has appeared in *Financial Times, Left Business Observer, Mother Jones, International Socialist Review, Diaspora, Socialist Worker, Race and Class, Monthly Review, In These Times, Z Magazine,* ZNet, and other publications. An activist based in Providence, Rhode Island, he is a member of the International Socialist Organization and the National Writers Union.

ABOUT SEVEN STORIES PRESS

Seven Stories Press is an independent book publisher based in New York City, with distribution throughout the United States, Canada, England, and Australia. We publish works of the imagination by such writers as Nelson Algren, Octavia E. Butler, Assia Djebar, Ariel Dorfman, Lee Stringer, and Kurt Vonnegut, to name a few, together with political titles by voices of conscience, including the Boston Women's Health Book Collective, Noam Chomsky, Ralph Nader, Gary Null, Project Censored, Barbara Seaman, Gary Webb, and Howard Zinn, among many others. Our books appear in hardcover, paperback, pamphlet, and e-book formats, in English and in Spanish. We believe publishers have a special responsibility to defend free speech and human rights wherever we can.

For more information about us, visit our Web site at www.sevenstories.com or write for a free catalogue to Seven Stories Press, 140 Watts Street, New York, NY 10013.

ABOUT OPEN MEDIA PAMPHLETS AND BOOKS

Open Media is a movement-oriented publishing project committed to the vision of "one world in which many worlds fit"—a world with social justice, democracy, and human rights for all people. Founded during wartime in 1991, Open Media has a ten year history of producing critically acclaimed and best-selling books and pamphlets that address our most urgent political and social issues.

Before and after September 11, Open Media has produced an array of anti-war works that focus on terrorism, "rogue states," U.S. propaganda, militarism, and the implications of U.S. foreign and domestic policies on human rights and civil liberties. These titles include:

9-11 by Noam Chomsky

Acts of Aggression: Policing "Rogue" States by Noam Chomsky with Edward W. Said

Bin Laden, Islam, and America's New "War on Terrorism" by As`ad AbuKhalil

Islands of Resistance: Puerto Rico, Vieques, and U.S. Policy by Mario Murillo

Media Control: The Spectacular Achievements of Propaganda by Noam Chomsky

Military Tribunals and the Threat to Democracy by Barbara Olshansky

Propaganda, Inc. by Nancy Snow

Sent by Earth by Alice Walker

Silencing Political Dissent by Nancy Chang

Terrorism: Theirs and Ours by Eqbal Ahmad

Terrorism and War by Howard Zinn

The Umbrella of U.S. Power by Noam Chomsky

Weapons in Space by Karl Grossman

Visit the Seven Stories Press web site for updated information and a complete list of all avaialble Open Media books and pamphlets.

openmedia@sevenstories.com | www.sevenstories.com